THE WOMAN ON THE FERRY

THE WOMAN ON THE FERRY

A Journey of 1,000 Miles to Redefine
Success and Discover Joy

BRENDA K. UEKERT, PHD

IN MEMORIUM

This book is dedicated to my amazing mother, Shirley Uekert, who taught me to always keep the door open to possibilities.

(October 17, 1932 – December 21, 2024)

CONTENTS

PREFACE

"YOU SOUND DEFEATED," my friend messaged. And yes, "defeated" perfectly described how I felt. My word of the year was "blockbuster." My book was supposed to be a bestseller. Colleges would line up for my speeches, and my summit would kickstart an EcoWealth movement. Instead, here I was in May, feeling utterly defeated. My book was nearly invisible, I had one paid speaking gig, and most campuses had "ghosted" me. The summit? A complete disaster by the numbers.

As I sat questioning everything, having poured my heart into projects that hadn't yielded the desired results, I wondered: Is success really about the degrees, the titles, the dollars, and the likes? Or is there something deeper?

Just four years ago, I had traded my suburban Virginia house for the RV life, crisscrossing the country and experiencing sights I had only dreamed of. I found joy hiking in mountains, watching sunsets, and waking to birdsong. The move paid off spiritually, mentally, and physically—but not financially. Last fall, I had slowed down, setting up an RV home base in southern California.

Turning 60 in December hit me unexpectedly hard, made worse by a badly sprained ankle in Death Valley National Park the day before. The reality was clear: if I couldn't make entrepreneurship work, I'd need a job. The thought of losing the flexibility of running my own business saddened me.

But then something shifted. What if this defeat was actually an opportunity? A chance to redefine success on my own terms? The catalyst came when a dear friend sent me "Squatter" by Yolanda Deloach, about a woman's journey on

1

Wisconsin's Ice Age Trail. Having grown up in Wisconsin, I felt deeply connected to the story. The book's "1,000-miler" concept sparked an idea: What if I hiked 1,000 miles in five months? For four of those months, I'd be traveling the western United States in my RV, seeking new trails in its diverse landscapes. This wasn't about thru-hiking one long trail—it was about discovering new places, one day hike at a time. The goal of 200 miles per month, about 6.5 miles daily, would push my limits on the wilderness trails I planned to explore.

Around the same time, I launched a Substack newsletter—*Nature Listening Points*—featuring my 60-second nature videos. It was meant to be a side project while I pivoted my financial coaching business. Then I discovered Julia Cameron's *The Artist's Way*. The book captivated me. What if, instead of relying on research and analytics to create income, I gave myself permission to be a writer, an artist, a creative?

I committed to Cameron's 12-week program, diving into her "Morning Pages" practice. Revelation after revelation emerged. When I started this journey, I thought it would focus on modern measures of "success" and finding different meaning through introspection. But as I embraced *The Artist's Way* philosophy, viewing myself as a vessel of the universe, I let the journey shape my book instead.

This book isn't just about hiking 1,000 miles—it's a quest to unravel deeply ingrained societal definitions of success. By immersing myself in nature, I aim to find clarity and reconnect with joy that's been obscured by the relentless pursuit of external validation. It's time to listen to the wisdom of the wilderness, rediscover what truly matters, and redefine success on my own terms.

INTRODUCTION

IN A SOCIETY that measures worth through external metrics—degrees earned, dollars in your account, followers gained—I've spent most of my life climbing the ladder of achievement. My story could be considered a classic American Dream—the farm girl who earned her PhD and created positive change in the world. Throughout my career, I've excelled at evaluating programs, writing articles, presenting groundbreaking research, and championing justice system reforms. By conventional standards, I had "made it." Until I didn't!

As I watched my business venture fail, I began to feel like I was living someone else's dream. In the relentless world of entrepreneurship, every business setback struck like a gavel, declaring me unworthy. The more I chased external validation, the farther I drifted from my true self. Exhaustion replaced passion, and clarity finally broke through: success wasn't something that could be measured in dollars or titles.

Life has a way of leaving breadcrumbs, subtle markers that only make sense when we look back. Years ago, a chance encounter planted the seed for this realization. It was a warm, breezy morning in the U.S. Virgin Islands. I was there for a work trip, my twelve-year-old child in tow, and we had signed up for a snuba adventure—a mix of snorkeling and scuba diving. On the ferry to Cruz Bay, I spotted her.

As we climbed to the ferry's upper deck, I noticed her—a woman with short-cropped silver hair sitting alone. She carried a quiet radiance that stopped me in my tracks, an inner light that whispered, "This woman knows the secret to life."

I watched her as we made the crossing, my gaze shifting between her and the breathtaking panorama around us. The view offered a feast for the senses—turquoise waters deepening into indigo, the emerald slopes of St. John rising dramatically from pristine beaches. Overhead, brown pelicans glided effortlessly, while frigatebirds circled against the brilliant sky.

She didn't just observe the beauty around her—she absorbed it. Every ripple of water and whisper of wind seemed to flow through her, her face glowing with a contentment that held the very essence of this crossing deep within her soul.

As the ferry docked at Cruz Bay, we made our way to the open-air taxis awaiting tourists. By chance, she stepped into the same taxi. When we reached our stop, she too stepped down. Following the sandy path, our footsteps aligned as we both headed to the adventure shack. There, in a moment that felt more like divine orchestration than coincidence, we discovered we'd signed up for the same snuba expedition. The universe, it seemed, was determined to weave our paths together that day.

During our walk on the beach, she shared her story. From the outside, her life had seemed like something out of a storybook. She had been married to the same man for over fifty years—a golden anniversary most would celebrate as a triumph. They had dreamed of retirement filled with travel and adventure. But when the time came, he planted himself in a recliner, content to watch the world through the television screen.

"I spent my entire life doing what I was supposed to do," she said, her voice calm but unwavering. "I played by the rules. I followed the script. But I just couldn't see spending the rest of my life in a rocking chair, watching the world pass me by. There's too much to see. Too much to experience."

Her decision wasn't easy. Leaving a fifty-year marriage seemed unthinkable to those around her. Her friends called her reckless, idealistic, even selfish. "Who does that at your age?" they asked. But for her, staying in that stagnant life meant dying a little more with each passing day.

So, she left. She traded the familiar for the unknown, the predictable for the possibility of something extraordinary. Now, here she was, walking barefoot on a beach wrapped in turquoise waters, her days filled with purpose as a volunteer for a nature conservancy.

"I didn't leave to chase some wild fantasy," she added, looking out at the horizon. "I left to feel alive."

All these years later, her name has slipped from my memory, but her story remains etched in my soul. She became a kind of touchstone for me, her courage a steady beacon I could call upon whenever life felt uncertain or choices seemed too daunting. Over time, she grew into something more—a mentor without ever realizing it, a quiet guide to a life unbound by convention.

As I set out on this journey to redefine success, I felt her presence more strongly than ever, like a compass pointing me toward something true. I finally gave her a name: Celeste. It seemed fitting, tied to the heavens and the vast, open skies she so effortlessly embodied—a name as expansive and free as the life she had chosen to live.

Celeste wasn't just a woman I met on a ferry; she was a reminder that the path to joy often requires radical courage. That one moment of radiance, that one brief encounter, stayed with me for years, surfacing every time I questioned what it meant to live authentically.

Now, as I embark on a bold experiment—to hike 1,000 miles in five months—I feel her presence as if she's walking beside me. She's the quiet voice urging me to trust the journey, to leave behind the weight of societal expectations, and to let nature guide me. This book isn't just about hiking; it's about the wilderness within us. By immersing myself in the trails of the western United States, I hope to find clarity and reconnect with a joy that's been obscured by the relentless pursuit of external validation.

Her words, or at least the ones I imagined she might say, echoed in my mind—gentle, steady, and sure. It felt as though she were speaking directly to me, urging me to trust the path ahead, even if I couldn't see where it led.

Let the trees talk.
Let the winds whisper.
Let the stars light the way.

1.

THE ACCIDENTAL BEGINNING

Dates: May 19 – 25
Location: Southern California
Trails: Pacific Crest Trail to Eagle Rock
Miles Hiked in Week 1: 52.4

AFTER SIX YEARS of entrepreneurial efforts—the intoxicating highs of launching new programs and the crushing lows of crickets chirping in response—I finally admitted defeat. Failure has a way of forcing you to take stock of where you are and how you got there.

Last fall, I had sidelined my nomadic life as an RVer for what I hoped would be a fresh start. With Los Angeles, San Diego, and Las Vegas within reach, I settled into an RV resort in southern California, certain I could breathe new life into my business and jumpstart my speaking career. Looking back, the irony wasn't lost on me: I'd traded the freedom of the open road for a stationary life, all in pursuit of a dream that seemed to drift further away with each passing day.

The vibrant life I'd envisioned had given way to the hum of ambulances in the 55+ community I'd tentatively joined. But then, Celeste began to appear in my dreams. Her radiance, her courage, her refusal to settle—they all resurfaced like a beacon in the fog. I could almost hear her voice, firm yet compassionate: "Brenda, let's be real. There's nothing holding you back. Look at where you are in life—you can do whatever you want."

Her imagined words sparked a realization: I wasn't in dire straits. Yes, the business had failed, but I was debt-free, with a solid retirement fund and no one to answer to but myself. I had nothing to lose.

Hiking had always been my North Star, a compass that pointed me toward joy and clarity, but I'd neglected it for months. It was time to reclaim it with an ambitious challenge: 1,000 miles in five months.

Then I laughed at myself. Here I was, writing a book about transcending external measures of success, and my first act of liberation was to set a goal based on—what else? External measures. But here's the truth: I can't quit metrics cold turkey. I love my spreadsheets, my charts, my goals. There's something deeply satisfying about ticking off a box, marking progress, seeing those numbers climb.

This goal promised more than just miles—it offered fitness, joy, and clarity, the very tools I needed to navigate this next chapter and redefine success on my own terms. Still, doubt crept in. Just last week, my total walking mileage was a paltry 4.6 miles. How could I possibly leap from less than one mile a day to my target?

1,000 miles in 5 months:
- 200 miles per month
- 45.5 miles per week
- 6.5 miles per day

I needed a test—a way to see if I was even capable of sustaining a pace like this. So I declared May 19 the start of my practice week. My goal: Hike the Pacific Crest Trail (PCT) to Eagle Rock every day for a week. The trailhead was just 30 minutes away, and the 6.3-mile out-and-back trail was the perfect distance. I knew this section well and loved it for its variety. The first stretch followed a flowing creek through a forest of Coast Live Oaks, the air cool and shaded. From there, the trail opened into the high desert, where cholla cacti and chamise plants dotted the rugged landscape. Finally, it spilled out onto an open prairie, golden wild oats swaying in the breeze like waves on a sunlit sea.

I started on a foggy Sunday morning. Balancing on a soggy log to cross the creek, I entered the forest. Two rabbits, looking up at me as if to say "Good luck," hopped away. I took my time, absorbing everything—the sun, the breeze, the babbling creek, crows nesting in the trees, and a lizard sunning itself on a rock. My senses were alive. Maybe I could do this after all?

On Monday morning, I woke up feeling tired and worn out. It was only day two, and already I was craving a break! I gave myself a quick pep talk, reminding myself that this journey would have many days just like this—days when my body protested, and my mind wanted to quit. Once I started walking under the vast, clear blue sky, I knew I'd find my rhythm.

As I entered the high desert region, my thoughts were interrupted by a sudden movement on the trail. A baby snake slithered across my path, and I jumped back with a startled, "Yowza!" I couldn't help but laugh at myself. Where had that childhood exclamation come from? I hadn't said that in years, but there it was, slipping out as if I were still a kid afraid of slithering creatures.

Tuesday brought companionship as I invited a friend to join me on the trail. We had hiked together before, so I knew our paces would match, and the time would slip by easily, carried by our shared conversation. My friend, ten years older than me and a cancer survivor, reminded me of something I often forgot: age is relative, and resilience is a lesson that never fades. As we hiked, her story unfolded—the end of a marriage, grown children, then finding herself living a solo life on the road. Her journey had a quiet power, a reinvention that felt so familiar, almost like the story of Celeste.

On Wednesday morning, I pushed myself out the door once again, bundling up against the chill that hung in the air. Alone but feeling a bit more confident, I stepped onto the trail and was greeted by a series of small surprises. As I crossed the cattle gate, I paused to take in a Coast Live Oak tree I'd passed every day that week. But today, beneath it, I spotted something unexpected: a cluster of Prickly Pear Cactus. An odd pairing, right? Yet there it was, thriving in the same spot, a reminder of nature's tendency to surprise us.

A little farther up the trail, I came across a wild turkey crossing my path. What a treat! I smiled to myself, feeling like the wildlife had become my companions. Even the cattle, moving cautiously away from the trail, seemed like old friends.

This was the magic of nature. No matter how many times I walked the same path, watched the sunset from the same horizon, or listened to the quiet breeze rustling through the wild oats, each day, each moment, was uniquely different. It was a gift, reminding me that the world was always changing, even in its most familiar corners.

Thursday's mission: test out my new pair of Merrell hiking shoes. But what started out as a routine hike, became an extraordinary experience. During the first two miles, I let my mind wander, flooding me with random memories, each one flickering by like scenes in an old ViewMaster. Standing atop Mount Washington, my father on his tractor, sharing ice cream with my sister—each image a thread in the tapestry of my life, weaving me into this moment.

And then something truly amazing happened. I slipped into a state of coherence, a perfect synchronization of body and mind. The click of my trekking poles, the crunch of earth beneath my feet, and the steady rhythm of my breath all merged into a single, harmonious cadence. In those moments, the weight of my past failures lifted, replaced by a profound connection to the world around me.

By the time I climbed into my Jeep for the ride home, I was riding a "hiker's high" that would stay with me all day. It felt as though my senses had been sharpened, each detail of the world around me suddenly vivid, bursting with color and possibility. The question lingered: Could I tap into this state of coherence more often? If I could, I knew there would be nothing I couldn't face.

Friday morning, I encountered my true obstacle: my inner weather wimp. If there's a weather excuse to be found, I'll skip the walk. Too cold? I'll stay in. Raining? A perfect day to curl up with a book. And so, on this dreary Friday morning, with temperatures hovering in the 40s, my first instinct was to stay nestled under the covers in my warm RV.

I delayed my start, waiting for the sun to push the temperature up a few degrees. Each day on the trail had been a surprise, and today turned out to be "cow day." I had to maneuver around a herd of cattle grazing near the path, their eyes curious but calm. I chuckled as I passed a pair of women further up the trail who had hiked up a steep hill to avoid the cows. Having grown up on a dairy farm, I felt perfectly at home around cattle.

As I neared the golden fields of wild oats, I spotted a familiar face—another hiker I'd crossed paths with over the past few days. We stopped to chat, and she excitedly told me about the bobcat she had recently spotted on her hike.

Her eyes sparkled as she spoke, and I felt another pull toward the trail—the sense of camaraderie, the smiles, the easy greetings exchanged with fellow travelers.

On my return trek from Eagle Rock, I was serenaded by a pair of house wrens, calling to each other from opposite sides of the trail. Maybe they were chatting about me, or maybe just singing their own song. Either way, I felt Celeste's presence with me, a quiet reminder that there are rewards when we face our fears—when we push past hesitancy, even our weather wimp tendencies

By Saturday, I was beyond excited to greet the morning, marking my seventh day on the trail. The weather wasn't much better than the day before—gray skies hung low, and the blustery wind made my hoodie a necessity. The trail was busy, so I hustled through the first few miles, creating some space between myself, a group of scouts, and a lively trio of women. My quick pace left me winded, but I welcomed the shift in energy as the sounds of birds and the rustling wind gradually overtook the chatter, bringing me back into the rhythm of the trail.

By the time I crossed the creek on my return to the parking area, I was overcome with a burst of energy. I raised my trekking poles in the air and did a little victory dance. I had done it! One full week of hiking every day! When I tallied my miles for the week, I realized I'd exceeded my goal of 45.5 miles, reaching a proud 52.4 miles. I could hardly believe it. I can do this!

SUCCESS, HOWEVER YOU DEFINE IT, REQUIRES A PLAN!

I'm a planner by nature, thriving on spreadsheets and detailed itineraries. My usual pattern involved nine to ten months on the road before wintering in South Padre Island, in Texas, but my extended California stay had changed everything. As I sat down to plan my hiking journey, reality hit: I had just four months on the road, not five. There was no way I could manage this quest in just four months. And after my successful practice week—with 52.4 miles already behind me—the answer became clear: my quest had officially begun.

As I thought about the trails ahead, I began to imagine Celeste's wisdom appearing to me in the form of postcards. Not real postcards, of course, but messages she might send from all corners of the world, offering exactly what I needed to hear at the right moment. I could almost picture her sitting in a quiet outdoor café, a warm cup of tea at her side, writing to me with a sense of calm purpose. I felt a thrill of anticipation as I "received" her first message.

Dear Brenda,

Greetings from this beautiful world! I'm so proud of your undertaking. Remember, success—like life—doesn't just happen. Make your plan, and then adapt with each twist and turn. Trust the journey, and you'll find yourself exactly where you're meant to be.

Keep going. Let the trail teach you how to walk it.

Celeste

Her words—or what I imagined she might say—lit a fire under me. A plan, that's what I needed: a serious plan to guide me toward my goal. But as I sat down to map it out, three challenges loomed large: low-mileage travel days, unpredictable weather, and—my arch-nemesis—boredom.

To get from one destination to another, I'll be driving my 32-foot motorhome, while towing a Jeep behind. Not exactly my idea of fun. It can be a white-knuckle affair that demands every ounce of focus. Add in the process of setting up camp—unhitching the Jeep, parking and leveling the rig, and setting up the catio tent—and the day's energy is zapped. With 15 travel days on the calendar, I felt a pang of anxiety. On those days, I'd be lucky to squeeze in a mile or two, let alone hit my weekly targets. The math was clear: I'd need to supercharge my mileage on non-travel weeks to stay on track.

Then came the wild card: weather. California in July could bring heat waves or, worse, wildfires. By late summer, Washington's skies would likely turn gloomy and wet. But not all was doom and gloom. The first six weeks of the journey looked promising, with opportunities for local hikes in May and early June, followed by a stint in the cool, shaded San Bernardino National Forest. If I pushed hard during those weeks, I could bank extra miles—a "reserve" to cover those inevitable travel days and rainy spells.

Finally, there was the monotony factor. I knew I wouldn't have the Pacific Crest Trail stretching out before me every day. Some days, maybe even weeks, would be spent looping around campgrounds or trudging along paved roads and bike paths. The very thought made me groan. So, I gave those walks a name: "Minion Miles." They might not have the grandeur of a wilderness trail, but they'd serve their purpose—keeping me moving and chipping away at my goal. By naming and mentally preparing for these less glamorous walks, I could stay focused, even when boredom crept in.

As I finalize these strategies, I feel a mix of excitement and trepidation. Celeste, that woman on the ferry, once a distant memory, now feels like a beacon guiding me forward. With each step, each mile, each challenge, I'm not just covering distance—I'm uncovering the person I was always meant to be. The quest has truly begun, and the path ahead beckons with the promise of transformation and discovery.

2.

SABBATICAL

Dates: May 26 – June 1
Location: Southern California
Trails: Santa Ysabel Preserve, Cleveland National Forest, Oceanside beach, Pacific Crest Trail to Montezuma Valley
Miles Hiked in Week 2: 56.5
Total Miles Hiked: 108.9

PLAN IN HAND, I was ready to dive into week two. After a week of daily drives to the trailhead, I found myself looking forward to some "Minion Miles"— walking the loops around the RV resort. It felt like a simpler, slower start, and that's how I began my Sunday morning.

As I made my way up one of the hilly loops, I met a neighbor walking her dog. Her husband had unexpectedly passed away just a week earlier, and as we talked, she shared how the dog still waited at the door, ears perking up at every sound, anticipating his master's return. Her words hit me hard, a stark reminder of life's fragility and the quiet grief that often goes unseen. Whatever challenges lay ahead in my day, they suddenly felt small and insignificant compared to what she was facing.

I instantly thought of my mother, recently diagnosed with stage four breast cancer. She was a spry 91 years young, driving to the pool several a times a week for her water aerobics class and meeting her gang of "girls" for lunch. Her future would now be filled with medical tests, uncertainty, and big decisions. While my brother and sister were able to lend a hand, I knew that I might have to leave the road at any time. Tears began to fall as I thought about life without mom. God, I was going to miss her.

As I continued my walk, I realized how much my self-imposed isolation—driven by the pressure to build my business—had kept me from forming meaningful connections. I'd spent months waving politely at neighbors and hurrying back to my RV, thinking I didn't have time for small talk. Yet here I was, chatting easily with strangers on trails miles away, while neglecting the opportunity for real relationships right outside my door.

Maybe these Minion Miles could serve a greater purpose. Maybe they could help me build a sense of community right here, teaching me to appreciate this place I called home—even if only temporarily. Gratitude, I realized, wasn't just about acknowledging the big wins or grand adventures. It was also about the small, quiet moments, like a shared story on a morning walk.

Monday was Memorial Day, and I was thrilled to accept an invitation from my brother to join him—and his two dogs—on an afternoon hike. I met him at the house he was renting temporarily, a place marked by the anticipation of his impending move to Colorado. Growing up, he was my role model, the one I idolized and tried to follow everywhere—from playing in sand piles with Tonka trucks to daring leaps from the hay mow. Like any big brother, he tried to ditch me at every turn. But the truth was, we shared the same love of outdoor adventure. Nature has always been our sanctuary.

With his move on the horizon, this hike felt even more meaningful, though I couldn't resist teasing him about plugging my RV into the 30-amp outlet at their new house. We tackled the Santa Ysabel Open Preserve, accompanied by his elderly German Shepherd, Angie, and the unstoppable Mia, his three-legged wonder dog. What a humbling experience! Despite her missing limb, Mia bounded along the trail like a seasoned athlete, leaving me struggling to keep up. As the slowpoke of the group, I was assigned Angie, who seemed determined to drag me up every hill. Occasionally, she would pause and glance back at me, her soulful eyes almost asking, *You okay back there?*

By the time we finished, doubt crept in. I was several miles short of my daily goal, and the realization stung. The confidence I'd felt the day before evaporated. How could I hope to conquer 1,000 miles when I could barely keep pace with a three-legged dog?

Back at the RV, I swapped my hiking boots for my Vibram toe shoes and squeezed in a few more miles. As I walked the loops around the resort, I felt grateful for the shoes and how they eased the strain on my knees and hips from the unforgiving pavement. Slowly, the day's doubts began to fade.

On Tuesday, I drove to the closest trailhead, reached through Dripping Springs Campground, part of the sprawling Cleveland National Forest. I'd hiked the Dripping Springs trail several times before, often with a friend, usually turning back at the three-mile mark. But today, curiosity tugged at me. What lay beyond that familiar stopping point?

As I stepped into the unknown, I could almost see Celeste giving me a playful wink, her voice whispering in my mind: "All the great mysteries lie beyond the familiar." Encouraged by her imagined nudge, I pressed on, eager to see what awaited.

The uphill climb grew steeper as the trail wound through a series of switchbacks. Enormous yucca plants towered beside me, their spiked leaves brushing the narrow path. The view from my perch was breathtaking—below me, I could almost make out the city of Temecula, perched between hills and vineyards. On early mornings, hot air balloons often drifted across the blue sky, though none appeared today.

At the four-mile mark, I decided to turn back. The descent felt like a welcome reward after the steady climb, and the ease of the downhill stretch gave me time to reflect. Back at the RV resort, I added a few more miles to my day, looping the familiar paths until I reached 10.5 miles. But even more satisfying than the numbers was the feeling that something inside me was shifting. I was beginning to feel stronger—not just in my legs, but in my resolve.

Wednesday, I coined a new term: "Mopey Minion Miles." That morning, I attended a meeting at the RV resort that left me feeling deflated, discouraged, and ready to give up my site altogether. Frustration bubbled up, and all I wanted to do was retreat into my RV and shut out the world. But I could almost imagine Celeste giving me one of her knowing looks, her voice playfully challenging me: "Walking might not fix everything, but it's a start. Go clear your head."

So, I briskly walked the resort loops, letting the rhythm of my steps and the familiar sights pull me out of my funk. With each lap, my mood lifted, little by little, until I felt ready to join an evening patio gathering with neighbors. As I stood among them, I reminded myself of a simple truth: a community is made up of its people, and I could choose where to place my energy. I didn't have to get bogged down by the negativity, gossip, or narrow-mindedness of a few. Instead, I could focus on those who offered smiles, warmth, and support—the ones who made the effort worthwhile.

On Thursday, I returned to Dripping Springs Campground, this time choosing the lesser-traveled Wild Horse Trail. Despite warnings of overgrowth, I discovered a completely different ecosystem—a canopy of trees, patches of orange mineral-rich stones, and a symphony of colorful wildflowers. Golden Yarrow, Thick-leaved Yerba Santa, and Mariposa Lily painted the landscape, while a distant creek brought vibrant shades of green into view. I paused to photograph the sweeping mountain views. By the time I reached the end of my hike, I felt a quiet satisfaction, thoroughly enjoying every twist and turn the trail had offered.

As I reviewed my travel itinerary, I realized it would be months before I'd have another chance to walk along the beach. So, Friday's outing took me to Oceanside Beach. The plan seemed perfect, but the reality of traffic quickly turned the adventure into a hassle. My barefoot walk on the sand was cut short as the tide rolled in. Afterward, I strolled the pier, stopping to observe the charred remnants of a fire that had decimated a once-thriving restaurant.

But even as I walked, I couldn't help glancing at the time, calculating when I'd need to leave to beat the looming crush of rush hour traffic. The outing felt cut short, my walk weighed down by the ticking clock. Back at the RV resort, I finished my miles on the loops, but the day left me unsatisfied. Time and traffic had stolen the simple joy I'd hoped to find on the beach.

Saturday marked the start of a new month, and with it, the countdown to when my wheels would roll. As I updated my spreadsheet, a revelation brought a smile to my face: I was on track to hit 100 miles today!

Excited, I left early in the morning, driving toward Anza-Borrego Desert State Park to explore a new segment of the Pacific Crest Trail. My plan was to hike the trail leading to the backside of Eagle Rock. But as I hiked, something felt off—not with the trail, but with my sense of direction. The further I went, the more certain I became that I wasn't heading toward my intended destination.

I'd messed up. Somehow, I was still on the Pacific Crest Trail, but I'd veered into the Montezuma Valley instead. I laughed it off, shook my head, and reassured myself: "No problem. I'll hike in this direction and turn back when it feels right."

The mountain and high desert views encouraged me to see what was around the next bend, but physically, something was wrong. My energy lagged, and a growing discomfort tugged at me with each step. At the five-mile mark, I turned back, piecing together the telltale signs of a urinary tract infection—a suspicion later confirmed with a home test kit.

On the descent, a small grouping of pebbles along the trail caught my eye. As I got closer, I realized the pebbles formed the number "100," marking mile 100 from Campo, the starting point of the Pacific Crest Trail. How fitting that I had reached my own 100th hiking mile on this trail!

Week two was officially in the books, with 56.5 miles completed—an impressive average of over 8 miles per day. In total, I had hiked 108.9 miles in just the first two weeks of this quest. As I looked ahead to next week's soaring temperatures and the need to treat my UTI, I felt grateful for the buffer these extra miles had given me. I knew the road ahead might tell a very different story.

SUCCESS IS DEVOTING TIME TO YOURSELF WITHOUT GUILT OR APOLOGY.

Physically, each hike made me stronger. But mentally, I grappled with persistent guilt. Who was I to dedicate five months to personal desires? My working-class roots whispered that success required hard work—not indulging in self-discovery. From childhood, I'd learned that worth was measured in dollars earned, and now here I was, stepping away from productivity.

I thought of Celeste. When I met her, I was consumed by career ambition. Her perspective seemed almost unfathomable then—here was a woman who had chosen purpose over practicality. Yes, she was older, retired, and perhaps her volunteer work helped offset travel costs or gave her a sense of giving back. But there was so much more to her essence. She exuded a free spirit, a quiet confidence in living life on her terms, an understanding that meaning couldn't be measured in dollars or status. That's what I needed now—not just her example, but her mindset, her courage to choose authenticity over expectation. I imagined a postcard arriving, offering her calm reassurance:

Dear Brenda,

The world says productivity equals worth, but nature knows better. A forest rests each winter, gathering strength for new growth.

Your "time off" isn't an indulgence—it's a necessity, like fallow ground preparing for abundance. Without these seasons of renewal, we deplete the very soil from which our gifts grow.

Remember that what appears as stepping away is often stepping toward something far more essential—your authentic voice, your deepest purpose, the work only you can do.

Take this time as the gift it is,

Celeste

The realization came gradually: I wasn't just hiking away from my past; I was hiking toward my authentic self. Like trying to hike in boots two sizes too small, my old definitions of success no longer fit. I found myself caught between societal expectations and personal truth. How often are those who pursue their dreams accused of wasting something—time, degrees, money, skills? It's society's way of keeping us "in line," labeling it irresponsible to step off the treadmill.

Then it hit me—my career could have been in academia. And what do professors get? Sabbaticals! They take time for exploring, researching, and writing. That's exactly what I was doing, even if my classroom now had hiking boots and trailheads instead of desks and lecture halls.

This shift reframed what I'd seen as self-indulgence into purposeful exploration. But as I released the guilt, I found myself face-to-face with a deeper wound that had been quietly bleeding for six years.

My life has been shaped by what I refer to as the 'Bermuda Triangle' of change—three wake-up calls that grew progressively louder until I was forced to listen. These signs appeared six years ago, though like a hiker missing trail

20

markers, I pushed on, ignoring each sign until I found myself completely off course.

The first wake-up call came after I experienced a glorious month away from the office. I had hung out with Master Naturalist friends in the Shenandoah Mountains, visited family in Wisconsin, and took a woodcarving class in the hills of North Carolina. I had a taste of freedom. My time was my own, and upon my return, my passion dimmed like sun behind storm clouds. I questioned my purpose: Was I making a difference? Was it time for someone else to take the reins?

The second hit harder. A colleague of 16 years stood in my doorway, her face etched with concern. "Brenda, I feel like I can't even stop by to say 'hi' anymore. You're always looking at the clock." She was right, and her words pierced through the hard shell I had created. When had time become more important than connection? How had I grown so unapproachable? In that moment, I hardly recognized myself.

The final moment—the eye of the storm—came during a late afternoon conversation with my boss. Without invitation, she claimed a chair at my table, her presence an intrusion. My hands trembled as I listened to her casually dismiss years of my work, each word another weight added to an already crushing load. It was clear nothing would change—the endless hours, the chronically understaffed projects, the leadership that undermined rather than supported. In that moment, something inside me snapped.

I remember it vividly: the weight of the ceramic cup in my hand, the sudden surge of energy through my arm, the arc of the teacup as it sailed through the fluorescent-lit air. Before I could process what was happening, the cup shattered against the door, pieces scattering on the carpet. The sound of the breaking teacup echoed the breaking of my spirit. In that moment, I fired myself.

The day after the "tea cup incident," I boarded a morning flight to San Francisco, the start of a two-week business trip that felt more like an escape. Despite years of resisting tourist trinkets, I found myself drawn to two items that screamed my unspoken truth. From Chinatown, an Alcatraz mug, its jailed prisoner etched inside, became a stark reflection of my professional reality. In Oregon, I bought a pair of socks proclaiming love for my job on the calf, while the hidden "Ha Ha Just Kidding" on the foot spoke volumes of my true feelings. One way or another, I knew it was time to break out. My job had become a prison, my boss the warden.

Upon my return to the office, I was ushered to Human Resources, where I was told my services were no longer wanted. It spelled the end of paychecks, health insurance, retirement contributions, and maybe most importantly, status. I had spent my entire life building a prestigious career, and suddenly, it was gone.

But when I look back at that day, the feeling I remember the most is liberation. Sure, I was stunned, and I would soak in bitterness for some time. The truth is, the image of that day is crystal clear: me, behind the wheel, a grin spreading across my face so wide it almost hurt, my favorite songs blaring from the speakers. As I sailed down the parkway, windows down and sunroof open, I felt lighter than I had in years. That joy wasn't forced or fleeting; it was real, raw, and deliciously rebellious.

Looking back, I carried the weight of my job loss like rocks in a backpack—each disappointment another stone. Over time, perspective emerged. The long hours and toxic environment weren't the root problem—they were symptoms of a workplace that no longer fit who I'd become. Being 'fired' was the escape I hadn't known I needed, like stepping through a door I'd been afraid to open.

Yet I had clung to that "failure," letting it define me. I wasn't the only one who had thrown away a career, but I had allowed that moment to shape my identity. But what if I had held onto that tea cup? Odds are, I'd still be trudging into the office today. Would I have left on my own?

I had planned to retire early, but not until I had more money. And maybe that's the problem—we "hang on" for one more year, waiting to complete a major project, waiting for retirement funds to bounce back, waiting for Medicare and Social Security. We continue working at the expense of our health and happiness, like hikers pushing on despite landslides ahead.

Is this success? To keep working for the wrong reasons? The truth is, it's what we do after an event that matters. How we respond to loss and hardship shapes our future. We decide which remnants of the past we carry forward—and how far we let them go.

As I watched the sunset paint the mountains in fierce oranges and purples, I felt something shift inside me. Each mile on the trail had brought me closer to understanding: I wasn't just hiking away from my past or toward my future. Perhaps I was simply hiking alongside both, learning to carry them with grace, like a well-balanced pack on a long journey home.

3.

THE WOMAN IN THE CANOE

Dates: June 2 – 8
Location: Southern California
Trails: Santa Ysabel Preserve, Pacific Crest Trail to Eagle Rock
Miles Hiked in Week 3: 49.7
Total Miles Hiked: 158.6

JUNE ARRIVED WITH a sharp contrast to May's golden days. The long-sleeve weather was giving way to an oppressive heat wave, and my UTI wasn't making things any easier. I knew this week was not going to be a walk in the park.

My health forced me to adapt my hiking plans. For five out of seven days, I found myself circling the RV park instead of exploring wilderness trails. My "Minion Miles" felt more like a hamster wheel than a quest for self-discovery. Up and down the roads I went, over and over, each lap a battle against both boredom and rising temperatures.

While this week's health struggle was minor, it reminded me of much bleaker times—a decade of managing chronic pain, back surgery, and the mysterious fatigue and neurological symptoms that had plagued me for the better part of a year. Now, I was in a good place; no excuses. Over time, I'd learned that hiking in nature was my keystone habit. When I hike, everything else seems to fall into place. My happiness increases, my weight drops, my energy soars.

To keep my mind engaged during these repetitive walks, I created small challenges for myself. By Thursday, I was photographing the park's flora, challenging myself to record varying shades of red and purple in the blooming flowers. Come Friday, I was reduced to counting birdhouses, grasping at anything to keep my walks engaging. These pavement miles might boost my fitness, but they left my spirit parched. My soul, I knew, belonged on the winding dirt paths of wilderness trails.

Despite the constraints, I managed two trail adventures during the week. On Monday, I returned to the Santa Ysabel Open Preserve, where a familiar trail presented itself in an unfamiliar direction. What I remembered as a welcome descent from the previous year now stood before me as a mile-long steep ascent through sun-dappled oak woodlands that had me questioning my choices. The trail wound upward through a mix of Coast Live Oaks and Engelmann Oaks, their ancient branches offering occasional patches of shade. As I got closer to the top of the hill, with Volcan Mountain looming in the distance, I began to struggle. My heart beat faster and a wave of nausea washed over me. I put my hands on my knees to catch my breath. I walked a few more steps, found a patch of shade beneath a sprawling oak, and rested. It would be easy enough to turn back, but I knew that the trail beyond leveled out into rolling grasslands. It would be easy, if only I could make it up this hill.

I couldn't blame the heat for my condition. My desperate state was most likely brought on by the antibiotics I had taken on an empty stomach. I slowly made my way up to a large boulder, a good resting area where I fumbled for my squeeze pack of peanut butter and sipped on my electrolyte-infused water. And that did the trick. Once over the hill, I walked toward one of my favorite sights, a lovely pond nestled in a small valley, surrounded by tall grasses and native oaks. The seasonal wetland created an unexpected oasis in the midst of Southern California's typically arid landscape. Later, I stopped along a creek, listening to the water gurgle down the rocks, a sound that would disappear come summer's peak. After the rough start, it turned into a pleasant 4.4-mile hike through this diverse landscape of woodlands, grasslands, and hidden waterways. Afterward, I met up with my sister-in-law for a stroll on the busy La Jolla beach.

I ended the day feeling a touch sad. This would be one of my last visits with my brother and his wife before they left California. And then the news came about mom's biopsy. The doctor recommended a mastectomy of her left breast. As a family, it was time to pull our resources together to help mom. Truthfully, I was beginning to feel the weight of upcoming losses.

By Saturday morning, I was determined to make the best of my time. With cooler temperatures, I headed out for a new segment of the Pacific Crest Trail just north of the town of Warner Springs. The morning held promise as I set out from the trailhead, the path winding through chaparral-covered hills dotted with granite boulders. But nature had other plans.

As I moved deeper into the trail, black flies swarmed thick as storm clouds, creek crossings loomed treacherous, and I lost my way on overgrown paths. At the four-mile mark, standing beside a particularly challenging creek crossing, I decided to turn back. The return journey became a battle of will against inexplicable fatigue. I had finished the round of antibiotics and had fueled up properly before heading out—trail mix, peanut butter, plenty of water—so I couldn't explain this overwhelming exhaustion. My legs felt like lead, each step requiring conscious effort. The sun, though not as fierce as earlier in the week, seemed to press down on my shoulders.

And then, something extraordinary happened. The buzzing of the flies faded, replaced by an almost supernatural silence. Celeste's presence seemed to materialize beside me, her voice clear as a mountain stream: "Trust in me," she urged. "The trail holds its own wisdom. You need only open your senses to discover it. Let understanding come to you in its own time. You'll find sunny clearings and wide-open meadows, but most of the journey lies in the dark shadows of ancient trees. These trees will whisper the secrets of the universe. Just listen. Listen and record."

The remaining two miles back to my Jeep passed in a strange, dreamlike state. As I finally stumbled into the parking area, something had shifted. The weight I'd been carrying—the doubts, the guilt, the fear—seemed to have lightened. I realized I wasn't alone on this journey. Celeste would be my companion and guide.

Despite the week's challenges—the heat wave, UTI, and modified plans—I not only met my weekly goal of 45.5 miles but surpassed it, logging 49.7 miles for a total of 158.6 miles on my journey. As I recorded these numbers in my spreadsheet, watching a red-tailed hawk circle lazily outside my RV window, I found myself reflecting on how often our perceived failures can lead us to unexpected discoveries.

SUCCESS IS BUILDING OPPORTUNITIES FROM FAILURE.

These physical challenges stirred up old fears—getting lost on a trail, unable to make it back, or falling like I did last winter in Death Valley. Even with my satellite emergency device, the what-ifs crept in. These fears felt familiar, echoing the paralysis I'd experienced after my career ended, when I'd sat day after day at my dining room table, my life growing smaller and smaller.

I remember those days vividly—the music in the background broken only by keyboard clicks, the view through my window never changing. Each morning I'd promise myself I'd go for a walk, each evening I'd postpone it until tomorrow. I ate too much, drank too much, thought too much. Fear had me trapped in an ever-shrinking circle—fear of failure, fear of judgment, fear of the unknown.

But gradually, something shifted. The fear of doing nothing began to outweigh the fear of doing something. I watched my life slipping away in that quiet house, and a new, more terrifying thought emerged: What if I spent the rest of my life just . . . waiting? The thought of that slow fade into regret finally became more frightening than any change I could imagine.

One morning, waiting for my hot tea to steep, I had a revelation. I could run my business from anywhere—all I needed was the internet. I didn't have to live like this. The sedentary lifestyle wasn't just making me unhappy; it was slowly killing me. "No more," I declared to myself, and for the first time in months, those words felt like truth.

On one chilly autumn day while visiting family in Wisconsin, I convinced my sister to stop at an RV showroom, trying to sound casual about what felt like a monumental decision. Row after row of gleaming RVs stretched before us, their windows reflecting the pale autumn sun. "Just to look," I'd told my sister, but my heart was racing as we climbed the metal steps into the first RV. The door swung open with a solid thunk, and I stepped inside. The interior smelled of new upholstery and possibility. I turned to my sister, unable to contain my excitement, and mouthed, "WOW!" In that moment, everything shifted. This wasn't just a vehicle; it was a new life waiting to happen.

Standing in that RV, I could suddenly see it all—mornings waking up to different views, afternoons hiking in national parks, evenings watching sunsets from my own little home on wheels. Sure, I had never driven an RV, never slept in one, never even set up camp. But for the first time in years, my lack of experience felt exciting rather than frightening.

Back in Virginia, I could hardly sleep. My mind kept wandering to RV layouts and travel routes, to mountain roads and ocean views. When I discovered my dream rig sitting with a "for sale" sign that December, it felt like fate. I signed the papers with trembling hands but unwavering conviction. I began renovating my new home the next spring, transforming it into "Goldie 17"—my business venture on wheels, named with a nod to my father's favorite number.

Piece by piece, I created my tiny home: installing new flooring, replacing the dinette with a home office, painting the walls a homey Broadway blue, and building cat boxes into the foundation of my new desk. Each modification made it feel more real, more possible. This wasn't just a renovation; it was life reimagined. With every change I made to Goldie 17, I was changing too—becoming someone who didn't just dream about adventure, but lived it.

I think about how I almost talked myself out of this life. I remember a friend asking, "what if you hate it?" I responded, "what if I love it?" But the biggest source of my worries? I had three lovely cats who would have to travel with me. Would I destroy their lives? How would they adapt? That spring, I tucked them into harnesses, and over time, taught them how to walk on a leash. Or in the case of the two little ones, tolerate a leash. I had to believe they would be alright.

Now, after years on the road, I see how failure became my compass, pointing me toward joy. Each "setback" pushed me in a new direction: losing my job led me to freedom, business struggles led me to mobility, and even physical limitations were teaching me new ways to move through the world.

This week's health challenges forced me to confront deeper questions about vulnerability and control. Out on the trails, especially hiking alone, there's nowhere to hide from your limitations. Every steep climb, every moment of exhaustion, every turned-back attempt becomes a conversation with yourself about what really matters. When I struggled up that hill at Santa Ysabel, or turned back on the PCT, something was different from my corporate days.

Instead of pushing through at any cost, I was learning to listen. To adapt. To find the wisdom in limitation.

The truth is, this quest of mine hinges on a delicate balance of good health, favorable weather, mechanical reliability, and plain old luck. Any one of these factors could derail my plans at any moment. But maybe that's the point. Maybe our limitations aren't obstacles to success but invitations to discover new paths. After all, if I could hike every trail exactly as planned, would I have discovered the subtle beauty in those RV park loops? Would I have noticed the varying shades of purple in the flowering bushes, or counted the whimsical birdhouses, or found moments of peace in the simple act of putting one foot in front of another?

That's when I thought about Celeste. A divorce signals a failed marriage, and after fifty-plus years, it must have stung. Yet, there she was on that ferry, glowing with confidence and contentment. And she wasn't alone.

As I hiked the trail at Santa Ysabel, the memory of another woman leaped into my thoughts—Dorothy Molter, the Root Beer Lady of Minnesota's Northwoods. During a visit to the museum in Ely that commemorates her life, one photograph had burned itself into my memory: Dorothy standing confidently beside a crystal-blue lake, walking stick in hand, leg propped on a rock, her loyal dog at her side. Her face radiated pure joy—the expression of a woman who had found her true path and never looked back.

Born in 1907, Dorothy defied her era's expectations. Instead of marriage and family, she chose nursing school. A vacation to northeastern Minnesota transformed into a lifelong love affair with the wilderness, where she became known for her homemade root beer and generous spirit. She crafted a life entirely her own, finding contentment in what others might view as isolation.

In 1964, what seemed like disaster struck. The Wilderness Act established the Boundary Waters Canoe Area, and the government condemned her property. Instead of breaking, Dorothy found creative solutions. When told she couldn't operate as a profitable resort, she set out donation jars. Her friends rallied with petitions, and she won lifetime tenancy. What looked like the end became just another chapter in her story.

As I pondered Dorothy's resilience and the challenges of my week, another postcard from Celeste seemed to float into my consciousness:

Dear Brenda,

What we call "failure" is often life clearing the path for something truer. The universe has a curious way of uprooting us from comfortable soil when we've outgrown our current container.

Your RV journey wasn't a retreat from life but an advance into its fullness. The freedom you've found on wheels has taught you more than any corner office ever could about resilience, adaptation, and joy.

Those who judge your choices are still measuring success with outdated instruments. You've discovered a whole new way to navigate—by the compass of your own heart rather than society's faded maps.

Forge ahead with courage,

Celeste

Dorothy found her calling and fought to keep it alive. Celeste had that same passion, that same zest for life. And I realized all of my failures were wake-up calls to find my true passion: adventure, the open road, and new trails to discover.

Looking ahead at my carefully planned itinerary, I understood I'd need to welcome the unexpected. To let magic climb into the passenger seat alongside my rational mind. There were many things beyond my control—health, weather, mechanical issues—that could derail this trip. But there were also many things beyond my control—breathtaking sunsets, mountain revelations, unexpected kindnesses—that might give me a lifetime of joy.

Sitting in my RV that evening, logging my miles into the spreadsheet, I thought about these three paths—Dorothy's, Celeste's, and my own. Each of us had found our way not despite our failures, but because of them. I understood something profound: every step forward on this quest—whether on a mountain trail or a campground loop—was teaching me to trust the journey. To see limitation not as failure, but as an invitation to something new. To recognize that sometimes our greatest defeats lead us exactly where we need to go.

4.

THE PRICE OF FREEDOM

Dates: June 9 – 15
Location: Southern California
Trails: Cleveland National Forest, Pacific Crest Trail to Eagle Rock, Idyllwild Nature Center
Miles Hiked in Week 4: 55.7
Total Miles Hiked: 214.3

AS WEEK 4 OF my quest began, the open road beckoned. After last week's heat wave, I awakened to a chilly, foggy Sunday morning. Though I had hiked 8 miles the day before and felt fried by the time I returned to my Jeep, the cooler temperatures and a hearty breakfast renewed my energy. I put on my jacket and headed to the Wild Horse Trail in Dripping Springs.

This nearby trail had become a favorite, showcasing nature's diversity—from the lush creek flowing in the valley to high desert terrain, from rocky slopes decorated with boulder art to mineral-rich orange stones. Below, vineyards stretched toward wild mountains. Determined to conquer a 10-mile hike, I knew it would be five miles uphill before I could turn around.

Around mile four, exhaustion tempted me to turn back. As I paused for a break, my thoughts turned to what was really holding me back from embracing this sabbatical: MONEY. I'd be spending, not earning. It meant dipping into retirement funds again. I found myself voicing my woes aloud to Celeste, complaining, "I am so tired of worrying about money."

And just like that, her voice answered in my mind: "Then don't."

I laughed out loud as I continued up the trail. "Then don't." Maybe it really was that simple? With my second wind and knowing gravity would be my friend on the descent, I pressed deeper into the trail. By day's end, including a trip to the grocery store and visits with friends in the park, I'd logged 12 miles—my highest mileage day so far.

Monday morning found me back on the Pacific Crest Trail, hiking toward Eagle Rock. On weekdays, this trail offered welcome solitude, broken only when I stepped aside for CalFire firefighters from the nearby station jogging past me. As I hiked through meadows of wild oats, I wondered about Celeste. Would she be in her early 90s now, bitter about her choices, or still that intrepid spirit inspiring others? Did she ever worry about leaving financial security behind?

On Tuesday, I put in some quiet miles looping around the RV resort, while my rig tested both my newfound financial philosophy and my patience. Just as the temperature peaked, the A/C suddenly quit working and the power quit. After checking the pedestal, I discovered a fried surge protector was the culprit. Thankfully, my neighbor, a retired electrician, came to the rescue. I was able to plug directly into the outlet until my new parts arrived, and he helped with the repair.

Wednesday took me to the mountain town of Idyllwild, an hour's drive from my resort. At the Idyllwild Nature Center, I discovered the truth in trail reviews warning about poor markings on the perimeter trail. Despite having my AllTrails app, I backtracked several times. The views were nice, but the constant hum of traffic intruded on the nature experience I craved.

Five days from hitting the road, I returned from Idyllwild to find my RV door jammed. With no way to open it, I resorted to climbing through a window using my telescope ladder—not exactly the adventure I'd planned for the week. Despite my acrobatics, the door seemed fine the next day but jammed again the following night. This time, I turned to an online community of fellow RV owners for advice. With their guidance, I took the door apart, adjusted the lever, and fixed it after two hours of tinkering.

Between mechanical challenges and mounting tasks loomed one final commitment—a presentation at a Los Angeles conference. The journey there revealed more than I expected. At 4:00 am, I drove an hour to the Oceanside train terminal, astonished by the busy freeway under the moon's glow. The morning train filled with commuters at each stop. A woman in a business skirt tapped away on her laptop, her polished nails clicking with each keystroke. I thought, "Thank God that's not me."

Walking from Union Station to the conference hotel, I passed through streets crowded with homeless people, many living in tents, using cardboard as mattresses. I watched people heading into work, pulling out their IDs on lanyards as they approached their buildings. The Los Angeles County Superior Courthouse brought back memories of my years working on court reform. Sirens wailed, and there wasn't a minute of silence to be found.

The workshop went well, with engaging discussions and attentive participants. But as I left, questioning how much effort to invest in this work, my heart spoke louder than any business prospect. Despite potential opportunities, I knew my spirit was already on the road. I had vowed to spend four months doing what I wanted, without letting business encroach. No more doubt, no more negotiations with myself—I had four months of freedom ahead.

I had walked miles on the concrete sidewalks of Los Angeles, and I was delighted to discover that I had reached 200 miles—and on day 26 only. I was averaging a whopping 7.7 miles per day. Last week, I had bought two Julian pies in Santa Ysabel, carefully wrapping each individual slice, tucking them in the freezer—a reward planned for every hundred miles, provided I had the discipline to keep them as treats. I dug into a slice of apple mountain berry pie, paired with a scoop of Tillamook French Vanilla ice cream. It was worth every step.

I had two more days left in the week, and a long "to-do" list to get ready for my travels. Haircut. Groceries. A new key made for the door. Stockpiling necessities. Loading up on cat food. Friday and Saturday were a mix of Minion Miles and errands. While these weren't miles for pleasure, they helped me meet my goals. Even Saturday's 97-degree heat couldn't stop me.

As Week 4 drew to a close, I had logged 55.7 miles, bringing my total to 214.3. My body had adjusted to what I was asking of it, my ankle held strong, and aside from minor tweaks, I felt great about my progress. The week had thrown its challenges, but the contrast between bustling city streets and quiet morning trails had only confirmed what my heart already knew: my path lay in the direction of freedom, even if that meant leaving some opportunities—and old fears—behind.

SUCCESS IS EMBRACING THE FREEDOM OF "ENOUGH".

In capitalistic societies, our very worth is often measured by bank balances and material possessions. But true wealth lies in the courage to step away from this mindset, to recognize that we can be rich in experience, connection, and personal growth. Success means understanding that money is merely a tool—not a measure of our value, not a shield against life's uncertainties, but a means to live authentically and pursue what truly matters.

Our beliefs about money take root in childhood. I grew up learning to avoid debt and to be careful with my money. Dad paid us for barn chores, and in the summertime, we earned one penny for every bale of hay that made it into the haymow. A good day was 1,000 bales, or $10 for a full day of work. The message was clear: the amount of hard work determined income.

But life has a way of shattering such simple equations. At thirty, with a fresh PhD and a contract to publish my dissertation, I thought I'd achieved the American Dream. Then the economy collapsed. Within months, I was downsized from my university position, setting off a frantic career search that took me to five states in less than four years. I was desperate, omitting my advanced degrees from job applications. Rock bottom was a cockroach-infested basement apartment in Atlanta, where the light in my eyes finally went out.

In that darkness, an unexpected spark ignited from the depths of my imagination. Kate Winston emerged—a fearless private investigator and the protagonist of my fledgling murder mystery series. She wasn't just a character; she was my alter ego, my beacon of hope. Where I felt crushed by life's cruel twists, Kate stood indomitable. Self-doubt plagued my every decision, but Kate moved through her world with unwavering confidence. Through her, I began to imagine a different reality.

Then life imitated art in the most profound way. As I crafted Kate's latest case involving local police officers in northern Georgia, I stumbled upon a posting for a Crime Analyst position. Soon I was driving an unmarked police car between offices, working with cases that mirrored Kate's fictional investigations. This job became my lifeline back to financial stability. Less than a year later, another door opened: a position in northern Virginia perfectly matched to my education and experience.

As I embarked on what would become an illustrious career, I marveled at the journey. From the depths of despair, through the power of imagination, to a life that echoed the very stories I had created, I had experienced a transformation that defied logic. Kate Winston, born from my darkest moments, had become the architect of my resurrection. In creating her, I had unknowingly charted a course to reinvent myself, proving that sometimes, the key to changing our lives lies in daring to imagine a different reality.

But the ghost of poverty never quite released its grip. Instead, it morphed into an obsession with financial security. I subscribed to a "save until it hurts" mentality. By the time of the "tea cup incident," my subconscious knew what my conscious mind failed to acknowledge: I'd be fine without a paycheck. My house was paid off, I was debt-free, and I could sustain myself for years.

Yet here I was, still gripped by money fears. Then I thought about my overseas group tours, which were fully paid months in advance. By departure day, they felt like "free" vacations. Why not apply the same principle to my journey? I could prepay four months of RV living from my retirement account to cover all anticipated expenses for the duration of the sabbatical. This simple act felt right, and immediately eased my concerns.

This financial strategy gave me practical freedom, but another kind of liberation was emerging. As I distanced myself from my business venture, I felt a surprising lightness. The pressure to maintain a social media presence vanished, and with it, a burden I hadn't fully recognized. I no longer scrolled through feeds cluttered with ads and promotions, each ad seeming to whisper, "You're not enough." By stepping away, I'd freed myself from that relentless messaging. In nature's quiet, I was rediscovering my own benchmarks for success and happiness.

As I updated my spreadsheet, I realized that the challenge ahead isn't financial; it was psychological. Can I embrace an abundance mindset, recognizing that money is a tool, not a talisman against misfortune? Can I redefine wealth in terms of experiences, relationships, and personal growth? As

I wrestled with these realizations about money and freedom, another postcard arrived from Celeste, her wisdom as timely as ever:

Dear Brenda,

Money is such a curious thing, isn't it? We grip it so tightly, believing it will keep us safe, yet that very grip can become the chains that bind us.

True wealth lives in the spaces between heartbeats, in the sunrise that asks nothing in return, in the trail that welcomes without judging what shoes you wear or how much you've saved.

Your freedom has already been bought and paid for. All that's left is to claim it.

Your abundance awaits,

Celeste

With Celeste's wisdom guiding me and the open road ahead, I was beginning to understand a deeper truth: Real wealth is found in the courage to choose experience over security, growth over comfort, and authenticity over approval. True wealth is the freedom to say yes to our dreams and no to our fears. It's having enough faith in ourselves to know that our value isn't in our bank accounts but in our willingness to live fully, trust deeply, and step boldly into the unknown.

5.

BECOMING

Dates: June 16 – 22
Location: Southern California
Trails: Pacific Crest Trail to Eagle Rock, San Bernardino National Forest (Bertha Peak, Grand View, Castle Rock Trail to Champion Lodgepole)
Miles Hiked in Week 5: 61.0
Total Miles Hiked: 275.3

JUNE 16 MARKED travel week, and I was beyond excited. Yet a part of me felt trepidation as I ventured into the world of Alone again. Would I remember how to hitch up the Jeep without consulting my "cheat sheet"? Would the temperamental RV jacks act up on the road? This week's drive would be a gauntlet of busy freeways and winding mountain roads. But beneath the nervousness bubbled an irrepressible thrill. This was it—the true beginning of my journey.

The Sunday morning air was crisp as I set out for my farewell trek to Eagle Rock. An early start rewarded me with solitude, broken only by a brief exchange with a fellow hiker who told me about turkeys ahead and a possible mountain lion sighting. As my trekking poles found their rhythm and wrens sang across the meadow of wild oats, I felt ready for the next chapter of my adventure.

Standing before Eagle Rock, I pondered Celeste's journey—she could have been consumed by shame and embarrassment over her "failed" marriage. Instead, she radiated energy and joy as she watched the scenery pass by on the ferry. If she could let go of society's judgments, couldn't I? Afterall, my losses— career, house, business—had paradoxically set me free.

Celeste's voice seemed to whisper on the breeze, "It is a BRAVE thing that you are doing!" The words hit me with unexpected force. This journey wasn't just about escaping the past; it was an act of courage, a bold step into an unknown future. As I placed my hand on the warm stone of the eagle's wing, I made a silent vow: "I'm done beating myself up. It's time to fly." In that moment, I felt the weight of old regrets and self-doubt lift from my shoulders. Descending the trail, I cast one last glance back, a laugh of pure joy escaping my lips. The path ahead was uncertain, but for the first time in years, I felt truly, completely free.

June 17 had arrived, and with it came that familiar cocktail of excitement and terror. It brought me back to the start of my RV life, when I was a complete novice. Back then, when asked about the experience of driving an RV, I'd quip, "It's 85% terror and 15% excitement!"

Those early days were marked by cautious vows: "I'll always stay in the slow lane," I'd promised myself. That resolution, like many others, didn't survive long. Soon, I was venturing into the fast lanes, giving myself a generous mile-long buffer after passing before merging back. Gradually, the art of navigating via side mirrors and judging the combined length of rig and Jeep became second nature. A year into my nomadic life, I realized with a start that the ratio had flipped: now it was 85% excitement to 15% terror.

In the morning, I walked a few loops around the RV resort before prepping my rig for departure. Connecting the Jeep to the tow bar went smoothly, and the jacks lifted into their storage position without a hiccup – small victories that felt like a good omen. Soon I was merging onto the freeway, heading north toward the San Bernardino National Forest and my 14-night reservation.

The journey wasn't long in miles, but it demanded every ounce of my concentration. Traffic came to a crawl on the freeway before giving way to winding mountain roads that required a delicate touch on the wheel and the use of turnout lanes. By early afternoon, I was pulling into the campground, a sense of accomplishment warming me as I set up my rig and the catio—my ingenious screen tent adaptation that allowed my cats to safely enjoy the outdoors via a ramp from the RV window.

The fresh mountain air, scented with pine, was an immediate balm. At 6,810 feet, the campground offered a refreshing respite from the heat I'd left behind. My cats—Coco and Isabella—seemed equally thrilled, eagerly taking up their posts in the catio to observe the local chipmunk population.

Tuesday was all about exploring and acclamation to the altitude—some hikes would take me over 8,000 feet above sea level. A paved biking/walking path accessible from the campground offered the perfect opportunity for an evening walk. As I strolled towards Big Bear Lake, the main attraction of the area, a profound sense of calm settled over me. Here, there were no name badges, no persistent ping-pong of pickleball matches. Just me and the soothing symphony of nature.

Each night, I planned the next day's trail trek. And with dozens of trails within a short distance, the possibilities were endless. I discovered I was the Goldilocks of trail selecting—not too short and not too far; not too easy and not too hard. I was after that middle ground of moderately-rated trails in the five- to nine-mile range. A routine quickly emerged: on days when I needed a break from challenging trails, I could easily clock five miles on the bike path, using the marina and jetty as my turnaround point. Evenings found me donning a light jacket for a loop around the campground, observing the varied camping styles of my temporary neighbors and greeting the dogs I met on my circuit.

On Wednesday, I geared up for a hike to Bertha Peak, its trailhead within walking distance from the campground. Mindful of the high elevation's dehydration risk, I dug out my hydration backpack. As I rummaged through its pockets, my fingers brushed against something unexpected—a sticky note, its presence both puzzling and intriguing:

The career is great. My social life is vastly improved. But there's a gap in my spirit. Something is missing. The adventurous athletic self has transitioned into a large lump who is feeling old beyond her years. I'm 51 and I'm about half the person I want to be.

I stood frozen, staring at this ghost message from my past self. The memory of writing it eluded me, as did the reasoning behind its odd hiding place. During the purge that accompanied selling my house, I'd scanned photos and combed through journals. Somehow, this entry had seemed important enough to preserve, yet its existence had slipped from my mind entirely.

As I hiked the steady incline of Bertha Peak's trail, transitioning to the steep, gravelly snake of its final half-mile, I felt a growing sense of physical strength. Reaching the summit, I realized my outings on the trails of the Cleveland National Forest, with their constant ascent, had prepped me well for this hike. I felt a surge of pride and possibility. For the first time since embarking on this 1,000-mile quest, I felt truly in shape, capable of conquering not just physical peaks, but perhaps the metaphorical mountains that had long cast shadows over my spirit. Far from the "large lump" I'd once lamented, my body had risen to the challenge with surprising ease.

Thursday came with a new adventure. I rented a sea kayak with the intent of circumnavigating Big Bear Lake. Pushing off from the dock, buoyed by the staff's assurance of calm winds and easy paddling, I felt a surge of optimism. Their only caveat—stay within the buoys—meant there would be no shortcuts to the other side of the lake.

Reality, however, had other plans. From water level, the lake stretched out like an inland sea, each bend revealing yet more buoys and more inlets and bays to traverse. As I approached Metcalf Bay, the previously calm wind transformed into a forceful gale, whipping up waves that seemed intent on thwarting my every stroke. I found myself paddling furiously, barely making any progress.

As I battled the waves, a fisherman on the shore called out over the wind, "Doesn't look like much fun!" I yelled back, "It's not!" Yet, stubbornly, I pressed on into the bay, even as the "Gilligan's Island" theme song began to play in my head. Finally admitting defeat, I turned back.

Revived by a meal and a delicious cup of my favorite ice cream, I returned to the RV and laced up my boots for a late afternoon hike on Cougar Crest Trail. This time, I opted to stop at the Pacific Crest Trail sign rather than push on to Bertha Peak, marking this route as my go-to for future explorations in the San Bernardino National Forest.

It wasn't until I began my descent that I noticed an uncomfortable burning sensation in my shins. In my preoccupation with the wind and waves earlier, I had completely forgotten to apply sunscreen to my exposed legs. The mild 70-degree temperature and my light jacket had lulled me into a false sense of security, causing me to underestimate the damage done by the high-altitude sun. I finished the day with a quick trip to the drugstore in search of sunburn relief. In the days that followed, my fears were confirmed as my skin began to blister and peel—a painful, visible reminder of my outing on Big Bear Lake.

As I reflected on the day's events—from my unintended reenactment of Gilligan's "three-hour tour" to my sunburned shins—I couldn't help but chuckle at the unpredictability of adventure. It may not have been the smooth sailing I'd anticipated, but it certainly made for a memorable start to my journey. After all, isn't that what true adventures are made of—the unexpected challenges that test our limits and leave us with stories to tell?

Friday morning found me on the Pine Knot Trail to Grand View Point, a 7-mile trek promising over 1,000 feet of elevation gain. The well-marked trail led me steadily upward, culminating in a boulder-strewn peak that lived up to its name. Sprawled before me was a vista that took my breath away—the expansive blue of Big Bear Lake cradled by mountains, forests stretching to the horizon. As I descended, I wondered if I had already seen the grandest view of my stay. Would the rest of the trails pale in comparison to this majestic view?

On Saturday morning, I nabbed a coveted parking spot near the Castle Rock trailhead. The trail provided no warm-up stretch, just a steep ascent marked by rocky stairs and imposing boulders. I felt like I was on a scavenger hunt, searching for the unique trail markers—large stacks of rocks encased in chicken wire. More than once, I resorted to the AllTrails app to help me navigate back to the path. Castle Rock was merely a waypoint; my true destination lay beyond: the Champion Lodgepole Pine Tree, estimated to be over 450 years old and 110 feet tall.

Beyond Castle Rock, the trail transformed into a dirt forest service road, leading me to the Wildlands Conservancy Bluff Lake Reserve. An old log cabin and stone fireplace spoke of pioneer days long past. The trail soon led me to Bluff Lake's mirrored surface, where I heard the gentle splash of ducks landing on the water. Sitting at the far end of the lake, I felt like I had stumbled upon my own private Eden.

I pressed on through the forest, marveling at the corn-like stalks of what I learned was corn lily. And then, there it was—the Champion Lodgepole Pine Tree. Standing before this giant, its gnarly limbs speaking to centuries of endurance, I was humbled. This tree had been a mere seedling when Queen Elizabeth I was granting permission to colonize the New World. It had stood witness to the entire span of American history, a living link to a past I could scarcely imagine.

As I made my way back down the trail, a smile seemed permanently etched on my face. The day had gifted me not only breathtaking landscapes but also a deep connection to nature and history. A profound sense of aliveness coursed through me, as if all my senses had awakened from a long slumber. As I hiked, I felt myself merging with the natural world around me. No longer an observer, I became a participant in nature's grand dance, my footsteps falling in rhythm with the pulse of life itself. In this wild expanse, I rediscovered home.

As I tallied up the miles for Week 5, I couldn't help but feel a surge of accomplishment. I had shattered my weekly goal, logging an impressive 61 miles. This brought my total to 275.3 miles. The trails had tested me, challenged me, and ultimately revealed a strength I hadn't known I possessed. I was in better condition than I'd dared to hope, my body rising to meet each new challenge with surprising resilience. But as I walked these mountain paths, something deeper was shifting—a metamorphosis that went far beyond the physical.

SUCCESS IS DARING TO BECOME.

As I considered my 1,000-mile quest and the challenge of writing a book with an unknown ending, a friend's casual remark caught me off guard: "Maybe you should plan for 10,000 miles instead. That'll give you more time to figure it all out." In that moment, the audacity of my endeavor hit me. Could I realistically expect to uncover life's secrets in just a thousand miles? The idea suddenly felt not only ambitious but almost comically presumptuous.

Yet, as I reflected on my journey thus far, I realized that transformation was already happening in ways both subtle and profound. Like my evolution from terrified RV driver to confident navigator, change was occurring with each passing day. The discovery of my past self's note felt like a cosmic wink, a reminder that this quest had roots stretching far deeper than I'd initially recognized. "A gap in my spirit. . . something is missing. . . half the person I want to be." These weren't new feelings born from recent setbacks; they were the continuation of a journey I'd embarked upon long ago.

Just as I'd found my sweet spot in trail selection—that Goldilocks zone of "not too hard, not too easy"—I was finding my rhythm in this larger journey of becoming. Standing beneath the centuries-old lodgepole pine, watching ducks land on Bluff Lake's mirrored surface, placing my hand on Eagle Rock's warm stone wing—each moment was shaping me, teaching me, transforming me.

This realization cast Celeste in a new light. Surely, she didn't transform into that radiant, contented woman overnight. Her journey, like mine, must have been a lifetime in the making. Each challenge, each joy, each seemingly insignificant moment had shaped her into the woman who had so profoundly impacted me that day. And now, as I walked these mountain trails, I wondered: Would I become the Woman on the Trail that people talk about for years to come?

And then, my thoughts turned to mom. Should I leave this quest and steer my rig toward Wisconsin? Mom's surgery was scheduled for July 3. I asked her how she was feeling, and if she wanted my help. But she assured me that my sister would be staying with her for three weeks following the surgery, and that my brother had volunteered to spend a couple of weeks at the farmhouse afterward. She was set. Admittedly, a wave of relief and gratitude washed over me. My siblings and I had been on a group call—we were all on the same page. Give mom the best days ahead, but don't prolong life if it meant endless hours of pain and suffering. We would make this transition as smooth as possible and ensure that she knew she remained in charge of her journey.

My evening walks through the campground became more than exercise; they became a metaphor for this journey of becoming. The path, lined with California Evening Primrose, seemed to glow in the encroaching darkness, their delicate white petals illuminating my way. Like my early vow to "always stay in the slow lane," old limitations were falling away. Each day brought new courage, new strength, new possibilities.

As these thoughts settled in my mind, another postcard arrived from Celeste:

Dear Brenda,

Standing before that ancient lodgepole pine, did you feel it? That whisper of becoming that takes not days or months, but centuries? Nature has so much to teach us about transformation—how it cannot be rushed, only lived through with patience and grace.

Like that evening primrose lighting your path, you're blooming in your own time. Some flowers need darkness to reveal their light, just as some journeys require us to embrace uncertainty before we can truly shine.

43

Don't just count the miles. Count the moments of awakening, the small unfurling of your spirit, the quiet victories that mark each step of becoming who you're meant to be.

With joy in your blossoming,

Celeste

The constant wrestle with my past failures had finally ceased its relentless grip. Just as I had placed my hand on Eagle Rock's wing and vowed to fly, I was learning to soar beyond old fears and limitations. The concepts of success and failure, which had loomed so large just a month ago, seemed as insubstantial as morning mist, dissipating in the warmth of a new day.

As I stood beneath a canopy of stars, a profound sense of gratitude washed over me. Gratitude for the strength of my body and the breathtaking beauty that surrounded me. But most of all, I felt an overwhelming appreciation for the courage that had propelled me onto this path of self-discovery, a journey that was already revealing layers of myself I had long forgotten. In that moment, under the vast, star-studded sky, I felt small yet infinitely connected to something greater than myself. Like the evening primrose blooming in darkness, like the ancient lodgepole pine growing ring by ring through centuries, I too was becoming—not just the Woman on the Trail, but the woman I was always meant to be.

6.

SACRED SPACES

Dates: June 23 – 29
Location: Southern California
Trails: San Bernardino National Forest (Pacific Crest Trail to Eye of God, Gray's Peak, Cougar Crest, Bluff Lake, Butler Peak)
Miles Hiked in Week 6: 61.7
Total Miles Hiked: 337.0

AS WEEK 6 OF my 1,000-mile quest dawned, I found myself standing at yet another trailhead in the San Bernardino National Forest, my trekking poles in hand. The week ahead promised sunshine and moderate temperatures, and I couldn't wait to discover even more trails in this amazing forest.

On Sunday, I set out to see the "Eye of God." A short drive to Baldwin Lake, just east of Big Bear Lake, transported me back into high desert terrain. The Pacific Crest Trail stretched before me, a serpentine path winding through the landscape. As I hiked, I paused to take in the distant mountains etched clearly against the sky. Veering off the main trail onto a dirt road, I spotted a few parked vehicles and felt a familiar twinge of dismay. Experience had taught me that easily accessible natural wonders often bore the scars of litter and graffiti.

A short walk down the road led me to the trail that would reveal the "Eye of God"—a quartz dome once revered as sacred by a clan of the Serrano tribe who had called this region home for millennia. As I approached, the acrid scent of marijuana drifted on the breeze, and I soon exchanged greetings with a couple smoking and taking photos. The juxtaposition felt jarring—this once-sacred place now a casual hangout for recreation. It seemed a poignant symbol of the destruction and disrespect we've too often imposed on sacred places and nature itself.

Standing before the quartz rock, I could only imagine its former glory. A century ago, before miners' dynamite had ravaged it in a fruitless search for gold, the "Eye of God" had towered over the lake. To the Serrano people, it had been the eye of their creator, the focal point of their creation story. Now, like the Serrano themselves—long since driven from their homelands by cattle-grazing ranchers and homesteaders—it stood as a diminished shadow of its former self.

After obligingly taking a few photos for my newfound acquaintants, I turned back, choosing a slightly different path that connected with the PCT. The rusted hulk of an old car caught my eye, its steering wheel poking forlornly from the weeds like a relic from a forgotten era. As I made my way back to the Jeep, the surrounding mountains captured my attention, their enduring beauty a stark contrast to the marks of human destruction I'd witnessed.

In the evening, I took a reflective walk on the bike trail, my mind swirling with the emotions stirred by the morning's hike. It struck me how age can soften the edges of our youthful memories. I could easily have been that 20-something perched atop the "Eye of God," joint or beer in hand, oblivious to the sacred history beneath me.

As I thought about my rebellious youth, I reached for the phone. "Hi mom," I said, "how's everything going?" My sister had informed me that the oncologist had recommended a mastectomy. Mom was already tired of the doctor visits, and confused about the information she was receiving. She swung back and forth—some days claiming that she did not have cancer, other days ready for surgery. But the one truth? Mom was not even close to throwing in the towel. She had too much living to do.

On Monday, I returned to the forests and mountains, setting out on Grays Peak Trail, a seven-mile challenge promising an elevation gain of 1,187 feet.

Armed with the knowledge that the first mile would be the steepest, I packed my snacks, gripped my trekking poles, and set off from the parking area with determination.

The trail, mostly shaded, zigzagged its way up the mountain in a series of merciful switchbacks. Overhead, a beautiful blue sky adorned with wisps of clouds seemed to cheer me on. Reaching the peak, I scrambled atop a boulder, rewarded with a panoramic view of meadows, forests, and distant mountains. Through gaps in the trees, I caught tantalizing glimpses of the lake below. Seeking a spot to rest and refuel, I found the true summit, a collection of boulders that required a bit of scrambling. There, in splendid solitude, I paused to take in the view as wildflowers danced in the breeze and a gentle wind cooled the warm air.

My descent began with a friendly exchange with another hiker, who relayed a rattlesnake warning from a couple forced to turn back. Either she had unknowingly passed the snake, or it had moved on. I hoped for the latter. Rounding a bend, I was startled by an approaching mountain biker who stopped to warn me about a rattlesnake sleeping in the shade about 100 yards up the trail. I was about to face one of my biggest fears. With only one way down, I cautiously proceeded, my eyes glued to the trail and my breath held tight.

Unless you're a running back in the NFL, 100 yards is a tricky distance to gauge. Just as I started to relax, thinking I must have passed the danger zone, I spotted a dark shadow by a tree. There it was—a diamondback, its distinctive pattern clearly visible as it rested peacefully coiled in the shade. My heart raced as I assessed my limited options: a rocky drop-off to the left, an unscalable ledge to the right, and a three-foot wide trail. Could I slip by unnoticed? Did rattlers experience REM sleep? Remembering that others had passed without incident, I edged to the far side of the trail and made a swift, silent dash past the snake. To my relief, it remained motionless, and the remaining trek to the Jeep went fast.

On Tuesday morning, I looked at the mileage I had hiked over the past six days, since acclimating to the elevation. I was astonished—58.7 miles, for a daily average of 9.8 miles—on very challenging trails. A text from a friend popped up: "Be careful. You don't want to burn out." My mom's voice echoed in my head, "Don't overdo it." They knew me all too well.

While my body was in good condition, I had to admit to a creeping fatigue. This quest wasn't a race. On the next day's hike, once again I stopped short of

Bertha Peak, turning back at the PCT sign. Even at this easier pace, I still had an 8-mile day. On Wednesday, I stuck close to the campground, taking easy strides in the morning and evening. There was so much to look at, with rigs and campers of all shapes and sizes, that boredom wasn't an issue.

After a couple of slower-paced days, I was eager to return to Bluff Lake, my surprise discovery on last week's hike. Armed with my GoPro and audio recorder, I ventured beyond the occasional casual hiker to my own private sanctuary. Perched on a sun-warmed rock, I let nature's symphony envelop me—the gentle splash of ducks landing, leaves rustling in the breeze, distant bird calls. I was in my own little corner of Eden. When I returned to the campground Thursday afternoon, I rented a bike and explored the bike trail into town, listening to the rattle of the wheels as I biked over a wooden footbridge.

On Friday, I took it easy, returning to those "Minion Miles" in the campground. As I walked, I ran through my trail options for Saturday, finally settling on a trek to Butler Peak Lookout. It would be my grand finale for the week—a 10-mile hike with a 1,630-foot elevation gain leading to a fire lookout tower. I set out early Saturday morning, unimpressed with the first few miles of fire road walking. And then, suddenly, I found myself in what could have been the Scottish Highlands—lush green mosses, vast grassy meadows, hills dotted with rocks creating an otherworldly vista.

Rounding a bend, I froze in my tracks. I voiced my exclamations into the breeze: "What! No way! Oh my God! You've got to be kidding!" There, rising before me in this fairytale landscape, stood Butler Peak—a rocky mountain reaching skyward to 8,537 feet. And perched atop this majestic peak, like a cherry on a sundae, was the lookout tower. A small structure with a wrap-around deck that seemed to hover precariously over the cliff's edge, it appeared both thrilling and terrifying. From where I stood, I couldn't fathom how I'd reach it.

In that moment, I felt like a child on Christmas morning, a mixture of excitement and nervous anticipation coursing through me. What an incredible gift this hike had become! As I approached the peak, I discovered a trail winding around the backside, leading to a blue railing and steps. With cautious determination, I ascended to the deck, one hand making contact with the building for security. The wind whipped around me, and I could feel the slight sway of the structure—a heart-pounding reminder of my lofty position. One lap around the deck was enough; I was ready to return to the relative safety of solid rock. As I began the long hike back, I found myself shaking my head in wonder at the day's unexpected marvels.

As Week 6 drew to a close, I had logged 61.7 miles, bringing my total to 337. I'd covered 300 miles in just 38 days, averaging 8 miles per day. The overachiever in me did a victory dance, even as that cautionary voice reminded me of the impending heat wave. I was more than one-third of the way to my 1,000-mile goal – a realization that left me both exhilarated and slightly daunted. Just as I had climbed to that precarious fire tower, each step bringing both fear and triumph, I was learning that the greatest heights—both physical and spiritual—require us to face our deepest fears.

SUCCESS IS FACING YOUR FEARS.

As I hiked to Bluff Lake, my thoughts drifted to my childhood, when my sole mission was to escape country life. I envied my city friends, free to bike around town and congregate at the baseball diamond, while I felt "stuck" on the farm, knee-deep in barn chores and summer hay baling. But somewhere down the line, things had shifted. The scent of freshly cut hay wafting through my open window, once the signal of a long work day, now evokes a wistful smile.

I've come full circle. The country life now calls to me—wide-open meadows, forest trails carpeted with ferns, the nightly chorus of crickets and tree frogs. I've been blessed to witness pristine mountain lakes, to inhale the butterscotch scent of a Jeffrey pine, to watch monarch butterflies dance in fields of milkweed. Here, amidst nature's wonders, I've found my true sacred place.

But finding this peace required facing deeper fears. Those country roads of my youth were synonymous with keg parties, where many of us began our drinking habits. Throughout most of my adult life, I'd abused alcohol. When I launched my RV life, I did it to save my life. Sitting at home, working on the business day after day, I had turned to alcohol and food as my reprieve. I was obese, depressed, and drinking too much. I had to make a drastic change.

Alcohol had cast a haze over my life, robbing me of the full exhilaration that life has to offer. I had thought of my ongoing alcohol use as a weakness, a lack of willpower. But when I reframed it into what it was—a habit—I was able to analyze the triggers and find a different set of rewards. When people ask why I "gave up" alcohol, the phrase always gives me pause. I didn't give up anything of value. Instead, I gave up hangovers, headaches, and hazy memories. What I gained in return was liberation.

Now, free from that fog, I can fully appreciate the beauty of this journey. The sunsets are more vivid, the cricket symphonies more melodious, and the forest hikes more exhilarating. This newfound clarity has become an integral part of my quest, allowing me to truly connect with nature and myself in ways I never could before.

Just as facing my alcohol dependency had freed me, the rattlesnake encounter on Grays Peak taught me something profound about fear's role in our lives. While our animal instincts serve us well against tangible threats like venomous snakes, what about the more abstract fears that plague us? Fear of failure, or its counterpart, fear of success. Fear of loneliness, abandonment, rejection, the unknown, and ultimately, death.

And then there's the fear of missing out (FOMO). But what if, instead of fretting over missing out on the party of the year or the latest tech gadget, we feared missing out on life itself? What if FOMO meant the fear of missing an adventure that could bring lifelong memories, wild stories, and unbridled joy? Perhaps too often, we let others' expectations fuel our fears. We worry about what friends might think if we no longer want to frequent bars, or how family might react if we quit a soul-crushing job.

I thought of Celeste and her bravery in starting over. How had she overcome her fears? I could almost hear her practical answer, "What was the alternative?" Perhaps fear itself is the catalyst for action. My rattlesnake encounter was a perfect analogy—the risk of passing a sleeping snake was far preferable to tumbling down a cliff. For Celeste, an uncertain future was preferable to the certainty of an unhappy marriage.

Reflecting on my own biggest risks, I realized the alternative had always been worse. Embarking on this nomadic lifestyle was a leap into the unknown, but the alternative—a life that drained my soul—was far more daunting. Yes, there's heartache and self-doubt along the way, but conquering fear eliminates one crucial element: regret.

As these thoughts settled in my mind, another postcard arrived from Celeste:

Dear Brenda,

Isn't it interesting how our biggest fears often guard the way to our greatest adventures? The rattlesnake on your path wasn't just a creature to avoid—it was a teacher about boundaries, respect, and the exquisite awareness that danger awakens in us.

Fear is like a shadow—it only grows when you turn away from the light. Bravery is not about being fearless, but about walking through fear, one trembling step at a time. The first step can feel impossible, but each one forward reminds us of our strength.

Those sacred spaces you seek often lie just beyond the territories that frighten you most.

Keep climbing, keep facing those fears. The view is always worth it.

With courage,

Celeste

One of the gifts of aging is the growing awareness of our patterns, habits, and sources of joy. The week had been a microcosm of this awareness: from contemplating a sacred quartz dome to sidestepping a rattlesnake, from pushing my physical limits to learning when to ease back. Each experience had taught me something about facing fears and making conscious choices.

The woman I met on that ferry positively glowed because she had set her priorities, freed herself from others' expectations, and conquered her fears. She understood that a life worth living is worth the risks. She knew that no one was coming to rescue her; she had to rely on her inner strength and go it alone.

As I prepared for the next leg of my journey, I felt a renewed sense of purpose. Standing at the Eye of God, I had witnessed how time and human interference had diminished its physical presence. Yet its sacred essence remained for those who approached with reverence and understanding. Perhaps that's what facing our fears reveals—the sacred spaces within ourselves, the strength that remains undiminished when we dare to look deeper. Yes, there would be more challenges ahead—daunting hikes, unexpected setbacks, moments of doubt. But like that rattlesnake encounter, each fear faced made the next one easier to handle. After all, isn't that what a life well-lived is all about? Not avoiding the difficulties, but consciously choosing to engage with them, grow through them, and emerge stronger on the other side.

7.

THE ART OF ALONE

Dates: June 30 – July 6
Location: Southern and Central California
Trails: San Bernardino National Forest (Cougar's Crest), Yosemite National Park (Yosemite Falls, Glacier Point), Sierra National Forest (Red Rock Falls)
Miles Hiked in Week 7: 39.2
Total Miles Hiked: 376.2

THE SAN BERNARDINO National Forest had been a slice of heaven, its moderate temperatures a welcome respite from the sweltering heat at my home resort. But as Week 7 approached, an unexpected email threw my carefully laid plans into disarray: my next reservation had been canceled due to a campground closure. Suddenly, I found myself scrambling to find a campground with electric and water hookups for the busy July 4th holiday week.

As I pored over my maps, searching for alternatives, the forecast for central California made me wince—temperatures were set to soar to a blistering 105 degrees. Yet this setback led to an unexpected gift. An RV resort just twenty-five miles from Yosemite's southern entrance caught my eye. While most of California seemed trapped in a heat wave, parts of Yosemite promised more merciful temperatures. The prospect of returning to Yosemite after more than three decades sent a thrill of excitement through me.

Eagerly, I secured my spot at the RV resort and snapped up some day-entry tickets for Yosemite. Then, neglecting my usual Goldilocks principle of moderation, I began to consider something more ambitious—entering the lottery for a Half Dome permit. The statistics were daunting: fourteen to seventeen miles depending on the trail, at least twelve hours of hiking, and a quad-burning elevation gain of 4,800 feet.

The decision made, I resolved to apply for a permit through the daily lottery. If luck—and temperatures—were on my side, I'd give it my best effort. But even as I felt the familiar surge of excitement that comes with setting an ambitious goal, a note of caution tempered my enthusiasm. I had to keep my overachieving tendencies in check. There would be no shame in turning back if the trail proved too demanding. The last thing I wanted was to jeopardize my entire journey with one overzealous effort.

Sunday arrived with a bittersweet taste. Feeling under the weather, I took a final walk along the campground bike trail, savoring the cool mountain air. As I dismantled my catio and prepared to leave, excitement mingled with a stronger emotion: worry.

With mom's surgery scheduled for July 3, my thoughts kept circling back to her. On Monday, I hiked Cougar Crest Trail one last time. Touching the PCT trail post, I whispered skyward, "Mom, I can't promise you'll be okay. But you have my love and support. Always." Speaking these words aloud somehow lightened my burden.

Leaving San Bernardino National Forest behind, I focused on the drive ahead. After navigating winding mountain roads—with my refrigerator spilling open on a sharp turn—I arrived at Bakersfield RV resort early. I spent the evening doing laundry, the shift from moderate mountain temperatures to central California's searing heat as jarring as my emotions.

Determined to beat the worst of the heat, I rose early Tuesday morning, departing just after sunrise. As I drove, I reflected on my good fortune—two weeks of mountain bliss with cool temperatures and breathtaking trails. I'd hiked my heart out, building up a reserve of "banked" miles that I knew I'd be grateful for in the scorching days ahead.

Arriving at the RV park in Coarsegold, I watched helplessly as the temperature climbed. My motorhome, with its modest 30-amp power supply and single air conditioner, struggled against the heat. The cats sought refuge on the cooler floor while the A/C labored to bring the internal temperature down to a sweaty 85 degrees. And then, I received news that mom's surgery had been called off—her medical team had failed to get cardiology clearance. This was going to be a challenging week, both inside and out.

Needing local expertise to salvage my hiking plans, I drove to the visitor center in nearby Oakhurst. The stop lifted my spirits—the center was staffed by a fellow hiker who armed me with maps and a list of hikes in the cooler parts of Yosemite. As I left, clutching my newfound treasure trove of information, I felt a renewed sense of purpose. The heat wave might limit the number of miles, but I was determined to get in quality hikes. I would rise early, drive into Yosemite's cooler reaches, and continue racking up miles. Celeste, I was certain, would approve of this strategy—adapting to conditions while keeping my spirit of adventure alive. Travel days always meant minimal hiking, and the day's 1.2 miles reflected the long hours spent on the road and getting settled.

Wednesday morning found me leaving under cover of darkness, arriving at Yosemite's southern entrance at 5:20 a.m. The booth was unstaffed—no wait, just wilderness ahead. As I drove deeper into the park, the scars of the Washburn fire from two years prior came into view. Charred trees stood as somber sentinels on the mountainsides, a stark reminder of nature's destructive power. Yet even here, life persisted. Tender green shoots pushed through ash, and wildflowers painted the blackened landscape with defiant splashes of color. Touching the steering wheel lightly, I whispered, "Life finds a way." The scene before me mirrored my own journey of renewal—how many times had I emerged from the ashes of my own personal wildfires? Financial struggles, the loss of a career, depression—each had threatened to consume me, yet like these resilient seedlings, I had found ways to bloom again.

Past the burn area, I focused on the curving road, heeding the "Speeding Kills Bears" sign with its graphic red bear making a compelling case for caution. Emerging from the historic Wawona Tunnel, I caught my breath as Yosemite Valley sprawled before me, framed by early morning light. At Bridalveil Fall, I found a prime spot and felt a momentary pang of loneliness—wouldn't it be nice to share this moment with someone? But as I stepped out of my car, the cool morning air filled my lungs, and I felt a surge of gratitude. I was here, witnessing this majestic scene, entirely on my own terms.

The day unfolded with a casual walk in Yosemite Valley, no set mileage goal in mind. I strolled to Yosemite Falls, stopped for breakfast, and meandered through shops and museums. Later, in what I can only describe as a moment of heat-induced madness, I decided to tackle the Upper Yosemite Falls trail. Half a mile in, struggling mightily, I had a little talk with myself. The heat, fatigue, and my own tendency to push forward, delivered a clear message: "Why push it? You can come back another time." I heeded the advice, logging an impressive ten miles for the day nonetheless.

My ambitious plans for the week, including a potential Half Dome hike, began to crumble under the relentless assault of the heat wave. Returning to my RV, I was greeted by an ominous silence. The power had gone out, leaving the interior temperature a stifling 93°F. After resetting the tripped power at the pedestal, I felt a wave of relief as the A/C sputtered back to life. But the close call made one thing clear: Half Dome would have to wait. I couldn't risk leaving Coco and Izzy in a potentially sweltering rig all day while I attempted the climb. Besides, my struggle with the Upper Yosemite Falls trail in the afternoon sun was still fresh in my mind.

Despite my reservations about the Fourth of July crowds, I returned to Yosemite at sunrise, setting my sights on Glacier Point and Taft Point. The two-hour twisting drive to Glacier Point demanded my full attention. At Glacier Point, I was relieved to find cooler temperatures, and breathtaking views of Yosemite Valley, Half Dome, and the high country.

The trail to Taft Point offered solitude, winding through magnificent forests and past massive stone cliffs. I paused to record a creek meandering through a meadow bursting with wildflowers, marveling at nature's ability to create such delicate beauty in this rugged landscape. As I approached Taft Point, however, the atmosphere shifted. The serene path gave way to a bustling tourist spot, the quiet melody of the forest drowned out by chatter and excited voices. Taft Point, with its lack of guardrails, offered unobstructed views and a sense of danger. The Fissures, deep fractures in the granite, added to the drama. Finding a quiet spot featuring a balanced boulder, I settled in for a solitary snack break. But it wasn't long before my peaceful moment was interrupted by a group of loud tourists. I retreated back into the woods, thankful for the quiet hush of the occasional hiker and the breeze stirring the leaves.

As I hiked back to the Glacier Point parking lot, I reflected on this internal conflict. I prided myself on being a responsible traveler, seeking connections with locals, honoring indigenous cultures, striving to be a steward of the land. But wasn't there room for all types of appreciation? And maybe, my perspective was based on my own solitude? Perhaps I would be one of those boisterous tourists if I were here with a group of good friends. This experience on the trail became a microcosm of my larger journey—learning to find moments of peace and reflection even in the midst of chaos, and recognizing that my way of experiencing the world was just one of many valid approaches.

Despite my love for Yosemite and its cooler weather, the long drives were taking their toll. Without a day entry pass for the rest of the week, I found myself tethered to the RV park. The relentless heat wave forced me to develop a new routine, one that balanced my desire for exploration with the necessity of self-care. Friday morning began with an early walk around the RV park, but by 8:00 a.m., the heat had already become oppressive. My body's protests and the scorching temperatures limited me to just 1.5 miles—a humbling reminder that sometimes success means knowing when to rest.

Saturday, I managed a short hike to Red Rock Falls in the Sierra National Forest, moving aside several times for local residents seeking relief from the heat. The oppressive conditions drove me back to the clubhouse in the afternoon, where I found unexpected peace in the simple rhythm of my modified routine.

Later, reviewing my mileage log for the week, I saw the impact of these adaptations reflected in the numbers. At 39.2 miles, I was more than 6 miles short of my weekly goal. Yet as I studied the totals, I felt no disappointment. Each mile represented a choice—to respect my limits, to prioritize safety over statistics, to adapt to the environment rather than push against it. My cumulative total stood at 376.2 miles, a testament to the journey thus far.

SUCCESS IS EMBRACING SOLITUDE.

As I wandered through Yosemite Village, memories of my last visit here, in my late twenties, washed over me. I had come then with a dear friend from graduate school, our Thanksgiving adventure a welcome break from work and academic pressures. That day remains vivid in my mind: loading the car under Oakland's blue skies, only to be engulfed by dense fog as we left the freeway for CA-120. Visibility dropped to near zero as we inched around sharp curves with deadly drop-offs, my friend clutching the door handle. We both let out a sigh of relief when we finally reached the valley and stepped into the lodge to register. Then, magic happened. As we exited the lodge, the fog lifted, revealing a canvas of clear blue sky. And there, as if dropped from a movie set, stood El Capitan in all its glory.

But it was an evening scene in the lodge that would unknowingly shape my future. An older woman sat alone with a book and a glass of wine, radiating such contentment that she caught our attention. My friend and I spun fanciful tales about her—was she an undercover agent? A holiday escapee? A widow reliving cherished memories? In our youth and inexperience, we couldn't fathom choosing to be alone in such a magical place.

Now, decades later, I understand what we witnessed that evening. That woman hadn't been lonely or lost; she had been complete, self-assured, finding joy in her own company. The quiet radiance she emitted was the same light I would later recognize in Celeste—the glow of a woman who had made peace with solitude.

We live in a world that equates being alone with being lonely, especially for women. Society sees a woman dining alone, hiking alone, traveling alone, and assumes something is missing from her life—a partner, children, friends. These assumptions run so deep that I wasn't surprised by what I discovered while researching Dorothy Molter, Minnesota's "Root Beer Lady." In a 1952 *Saturday Evening Post* article, they had dubbed her "The Loneliest Woman in America," as if a woman choosing solitude must surely be suffering. Yet when asked about her isolation years later, Dorothy's response was simple yet profound: "I never get lonely in winter when I am alone." Her words cut through decades of societal assumptions about solitude and womanhood.

Dorothy's story mirrors my own evolving relationship with solitude. Like her, I'm discovering that being alone doesn't mean being lonely. I find myself drawing strength from an unexpected sisterhood: Dorothy tending her wilderness home, Celeste stepping boldly into her next chapter, the Woman in the Lodge savoring her book in perfect contentment. These women weren't marking time or making do; they were living fully, vibrantly, on their own terms They had discovered something profound: that a life lived on one's own terms, embracing solitude rather than fighting it, could be rich beyond measure.

As I pondered these thoughts, another postcard arrived from Celeste:

Dear Brenda,

Isn't it fascinating how society confuses solitude with loneliness? They see a woman alone and assume something is missing, like a symphony with a silent instrument. But you and I know better—sometimes that silence itself is the most profound music.

You're discovering now what I learned later in life—that true companionship begins with befriending yourself. Every solo hike, every quiet moment, every challenge faced alone adds another thread to the tapestry of who you are becoming.

Embrace these moments of solitude. They're not empty spaces to be filled, but sacred grounds where your spirit can truly flourish.

With peaceful solidarity,

Celeste

The wisdom in Celeste's words resonated deeply. My journey was teaching me that solitude isn't something to be endured but a gift to be cherished. In these moments alone—whether standing breathless before Yosemite's grandeur or seeking refuge from the heat in a quiet clubhouse—I was discovering that the art of being alone requires practice, patience, and a willingness to sit with oneself, embracing all complexities and contradictions.

I thought about how far I'd come from those early days of RV life, when solitude felt more like exile than liberation. Now, I find myself savoring the simplest pleasures—a purring cat on my lap, the perfect cup of Earl Grey tea, the sun painting the mountains in soft morning light. These quiet moments, once overlooked in the rush of "normal" life, have become the foundation of my happiness.

As I prepared for sleep, I felt a sense of completion. I was honoring the woman I had become, the one who had learned to find wholeness in herself. In the quiet of the night, I understood that true success wasn't measured in miles hiked or mountains climbed, but in the courage to embrace our own company and find joy in the journey, wherever it leads.

8.

UNBECOMING

Dates: July 7 – 13
Location: Central California and South-Central Oregon
Trails: Yosemite National Park (Chilnualna Falls), Crater Lake National Park (Wizard Island Trail), Rogue River-Siskiyou National Forest (Pearsony Falls, Natural Bridge, Takelma Gorge)
Miles Hiked in Week 8: 32.5
Total Miles Hiked: 408.7

THAT FIRST SUNDAY of week 8, with temperatures soaring to 108 degrees, I found myself surrendering to the heat, too drained for my usual morning hike. The cats and I settled for gentle moments in the pre-dawn hours—them exploring on their leashes, me guiding—before retreating to the air-conditioned sanctuary of the clubhouse as the day blazed to life. I managed just over a mile, a far cry from my daily goal, but sometimes wisdom means adapting rather than pushing forward for the sake of a number.

On Monday, I was determined to get in one last hike in Yosemite, despite the heat. I left early in the morning, set on reaching the trailhead to Chilnualna Falls, located in the southern part of the park. My 20-minute wait in the line of cars at the entrance delayed my start, and the day was heating up quickly.

As I reached the trailhead, I glanced at the route on my app—a 4-mile ascent to the upper falls. It didn't take long to reach the lower falls, and I stopped to take in the view. While most of the trail was shade-covered, I could feel the full strength of the sun on the exposed patches of rocky areas. As I hiked further, I began to feel the telltale signs of hay fever. I used my app to identify the plants surrounding the trail and laughed when I discovered the generic name of the plant causing my grief was Mountain Misery. Perfect!

I met a pair of young hikers on the trail, and we ended up leapfrogging each other on the ascent. As the temperature climbed, they would step off the trail to catch a break, and I would pass. Then it was my turn to take a break, and they would pass me. Finally, I reached a viewpoint of the upper falls. I looked ahead and saw that the trail wound further, but there was little shade. I asked a descending hiker how much further before reaching the falls, and he indicated it was "just around the bend." My energy was zapped, so I sat on a rock, eating my snack before tackling the last part of the trail.

With renewed energy, I climbed up rocky steps, and hopped off trail to find a resting place on the rocks by the stream of water that flowed between the upper and lower falls. This was heavenly. I had the place to myself and I pulled out my GoPro to make an extended video, featuring the flowing water before it cascaded down the rockface into another falls. Before I started the descent, I dipped my hat and Columbia sunscreen shirt in the creek, letting the cool water pour down my body. I had one more bottle of water to make it to the bottom and hoped gravity would speed up the journey. Halfway down, I found more running water and repeated my cooldown method.

As I neared the end of my hike, I began dreaming about a bottle of ice-cold water and was thankful for the little store I had passed on my way to the falls. When I checked the temperature at the parking area, it was 100 degrees. It was a challenging but rewarding end to my Yosemite adventure.

As Tuesday dawned, I pointed my RV northward, to the city of Corning, where an urban RV resort promised a brief respite from the road. The day's blistering temperatures kept me from venturing outside. As the evening brought cooler temperatures, I rushed outside to hang a damp item on the picnic table. Turning back, I saw the RV door ajar and a flash of fur as Coco (aka "Houdini") made her escape.

What followed was an hour-long comedy of errors that would have made any cat herder proud. Coco led me on a merry chase around the campground, finally scaling a tree in hot pursuit of a bird. My heart lodged in my throat as I watched her speedy descent, reminded once again why "herding cats" is synonymous with impossibility.

As darkness approached, I changed tactics. I harnessed Isabella, hoping her presence might lure our escapee home. Together, we waited by the open RV door. True to her mischievous nature, Coco finally returned, leaping into the RV as if her rendezvous with nature were no big deal!

Wednesday was another push north into Oregon. As I approached the border, I was stunned to see the snow-capped peak of Mount Shasta emerging on the horizon. That afternoon, my arrival at the RV park coincided with a power outage, which could have been disastrous, were it not for the towering conifers shading my campsite.

Setting up camp for my 10-day stay, I nudged the picnic table aside to make room for the catio. As I let Coco and Isabella out to play in their safe space, I smiled as I saw a chipmunk peer out from a tree, knowing the cats would be well entertained. Exploring the campground, I felt a surge of anticipation for the discoveries that lay ahead.

I awoke Thursday morning with a sense of childlike excitement, as if it were Christmas morning and I couldn't wait to see what Santa left under the tree. I had a reservation on a combo boat tour that would set me on Wizard Island, a volcanic cinder cone at the west end of Crater Lake. As I drove into the park and looked over the rim for the first time, I felt tears roll down my cheeks. I have never seen such clear cobalt waters shimmering in the sun, and the sight took my breath away. I had just left majestic Yosemite National Park, and here I was about to set foot in more spectacular scenery.

The intensity of my emotional reaction caught me off guard. It wasn't just the beauty of the lake that moved me to tears, but the realization of how far I'd come on this journey. Standing there, I felt a profound connection to the Earth. It was as if the lake's pristine waters were reflecting not just the sky, but my own transformation. I thought of Celeste, and wondered if this was the kind of awe she felt when she first arrived on the island. In that moment, I understood why some consider nature to be sacred—it has the power to strip away our pretenses and connect us to something greater than ourselves.

I wound my way to the parking area, checked in for the boat tour, and hiked down the steep switchback Cleetwood Cove trail to the boat dock. Aboard the tour boat, our guide told us about Mount Mazama, a large complex volcano, erupted violently almost 8,000 years ago, forming its caldera which now contains Crater Lake. I marveled at the blue skies, the deep blue color of the water, and the snow-capped peaks.

Once on Wizard Island, I climbed the snaking trail to the summit, where I looked into the crater (the "Witches Cauldron") to discover not just snow, but a snow slide. I felt like I was in a movie scene as I watched a couple take turns sliding down, shouting with glee as they went. I walked the rim, but with time running out, I hurried down the trail, carefully walking over fields of giant lava rocks to get a glance at Fumarole Bay, watching people laugh and swim in the chilly waters. What an amazing gift to witness the incredulous beauty of nature.

Before leaving the island, I called out to a stranger standing on the dock. He was wearing a red t-shirt boldly declaring "Choose FI." I recognized the acronym instantly – Choose Financial Independence. And that's how I met Mitch, who was on a summer sabbatical with his family. He'd recently traded a high-level executive position for a less stressful, hands-on role—this trip marking his transition between the two. Our virtual friendship evolved into a tangible opportunity when Mitch, now hosting a podcast on financial independence, invited me as a guest. It's these mysterious connections that keep life interesting.

Once aboard the boat for the remainder of our tour, our guide shared that Crater Lake, at 1,943 feet deep, is the deepest lake in the United States and the deepest volcanic lake in the world. And the blue color? It's due to the depth and purity of the water—it has no sediments, algae, or pollutants and it absorbs all of the colors of the color spectrum except the blues. Our guide then demonstrated by filling our water bottles with water directly from the lake—I half expected the color to be blue! It was a spectacular and moving day.

As the week approached its end, I stuck closer to the RV resort, exploring local sights and trails. I set Friday aside to visit some of the waterfalls within a few miles of the campground. My first stop was Pearsony Falls, with its gentle cascading waters. I recorded three more waterfalls and was about to call it quits when I discovered a sign pointing to the Natural Bridge. I couldn't resist. Here, I witnessed the amazing Rogue River flowing through a lava tube!

On Saturday, the temperature reached 100 degrees. I left the RV early and drove 15 minutes to find Woodward Bridge in the Rogue River-Siskiyou

National Forest. From there, I hiked several miles to the Takelma Gorge, stopping to ponder the strength of the river as it carved out the gorge. The water pounded in my ears, and I stepped carefully on the lava rock that formed the trail bed over part of the gorge. I was the only person on the trail, and was enthralled by the mysteries of the Rogue River, from its thundering whitewater to its quieter serene sections.

Later, tallying my miles for the week, I saw the impact of travel days and scorching temperatures reflected in my lowest weekly total yet—just 32.5 miles, leaving me 13 miles short of my weekly goal. Yet my early dedication to "banking" extra miles had proven wise; my cumulative total stood at 408.7 miles, well ahead of schedule. But something more significant than numbers was emerging. As I sat in my campsite beneath towering conifers, listening to the evening chorus of birds and watching chipmunks scamper past my catio, I realized that this week's journey—from Yosemite's majestic waterfalls to Crater Lake's pristine waters—had shifted something profound within me.

SUCCESS IS UNBECOMING.

Standing at the rim of Crater Lake, tears streaming down my face at the sight of those impossibly blue waters, I began to understand that nature wasn't just my playground—it was my sanctuary, my teacher, and the key to unlocking a more authentic version of myself. Like the volcanic forces that had shaped this landscape, transformative powers were at work within me, breaking down old structures to create something new.

I realized that I had been laser-focused on becoming more like Celeste. But what I had neglected was the opposite process—unbecoming. To live my own life the way I want, to be authentic, meant going against the norm, a conventional life as defined by society. Truthfully, that simple act I took months ago—prepaying my rent and travel expenses—unburdened my mind from their old worries about money. And now, I was creating space for something more authentic to emerge.

As I contemplated this concept of "unbecoming," I couldn't help but think of mom's parallel journey. Her email arrived with heartbreaking timing: "Some days, I don't even know who I am anymore. . . . my life was so simple before this all began. I am trying hard to adapt." With her surgery rescheduled for July 31 and more appointments ahead, she was worn out, mentally and emotionally.

She had convinced herself that she now needed heart surgery, even though we had told her that wasn't the case. By mid-week, we had received results from her CT scan—a mass on her lung and enlarged lymph nodes. In our phone call, she told me, "what's strange is that I never have any pain." Mom was being forced into her own form of unbecoming, shedding her identity as a healthy, independent woman, while I was voluntarily shedding societal expectations.

As a woman in America, I'd been shaped by countless warnings and restrictions—don't hike alone, don't talk to strangers, blend in, stay safe. The lessons from my conservative rural Lutheran upbringing had taught me about the subservience of women, where women couldn't serve on the church council, couldn't usher, couldn't be ministers, couldn't even vote on church matters. I fled that institution at the age of eighteen, but its walls and borders had already left their mark. Like sedimentary layers of rock, these expectations had accumulated over time, each one pressing down on the ones before, until the weight of them all threatened to crush whatever lay beneath.

But nature knows something about pressure and transformation. Just as heat and pressure turn coal into diamonds, the pressure of conforming to society's expectations had ultimately fueled my rebellion. Each restriction became a reason to push back, each "should" and "must" an invitation to question why. The heat of my discontent had slowly transformed me, making me harder in some ways but also more precious to myself.

This process of unbecoming is both liberating and terrifying. Each time I shed a layer of societal expectation, I feel lighter, more authentic. But it also exposes vulnerabilities I've long kept hidden. Like a hermit crab between shells, there are moments of complete exposure, moments when I feel raw and unprotected. Yet these are also the moments when growth becomes possible.

Years ago, while clinging to my high-stress career, I'd read about the four spheres of life: work, play, love, and health. The inclusion of play as a major sphere had struck me as foreign—who had time for play when there were responsibilities to meet? Like many Americans, I'd relegated play to scheduled vacation days and occasional weekend outings. Play was something you earned through work, not a vital part of daily existence.

But nature doesn't separate work from play. A river doesn't clock in to carve its canyon. Trees don't schedule their growth. Ravens don't pencil in time for aerial acrobatics. Watching the couple slide down the snow bank in Wizard Island's crater, their laughter echoing across the caldera, I saw how artificial these divisions were. Their spontaneous joy reminded me of something I'd lost along the way—the ability to be fully present in a moment, to find delight in simple things.

Unbecoming, I realized, is largely about unlearning—especially our complicated relationship with time. We partition our lives into segments: work time, family time, me time. We set alarms, create schedules, live by calendars. But out here on the trail, time flows differently. Like the Rogue River finding its path through the lava tube at Natural Bridge, it follows its own course. Some days stretch out endlessly; others compress into a handful of vivid moments. The only schedule that matters is the rhythm of sunrise and sunset, the dance of weather systems, the pulse of my own energy rising and falling.

Perhaps this is why my tears at Crater Lake caught me so off guard. They weren't just about the beauty before me; they were a release of something deeper. In that moment, I felt myself touching an ancient truth—that we are not separate from nature but part of it. All our careful constructions of identity, our professional titles, our social roles, our carefully curated online personas— these are just layers of sediment covering our true selves.

As I pondered these transformations, another postcard arrived from Celeste:

Dear Brenda,

Isn't it beautiful to witness your own unbecoming? Like watching a butterfly emerge from its chrysalis, there's both vulnerability and strength in the process. Society wraps us in layers of "should" and "must," but nature knows better. She shows us that transformation is natural, that breaking free is part of growth.

I see you discovering what I found on my island—that joy isn't something to pursue but something to notice, like the way sunlight dances on water or how wind whispers through trees. Every tear you shed at Crater Lake was washing away another layer of who you were told to be, revealing who you've always been.

Remember, a waterfall doesn't question its path or apologize for its power. Neither should you.

Flow freely,

Celeste

Celeste's words resonated deeply as I reflected on nature's own lessons in unbecoming. The resilience of a tree growing from a crack in a rock face, the patience of water carving a canyon over millennia, the interconnectedness of forest ecosystems—these are not just poetic metaphors, but blueprints for transformation. Nature shows us that growth isn't always about adding; sometimes it's about wearing away what doesn't serve us, like water smoothing stone.

These lessons in letting go challenged everything I'd believed about success and legacy. My career used to feed my sense of purpose, and I thought it would be my legacy. But when I left the workplace, I discovered that a legacy isn't a thing we leave behind—not a business, a product, or an inheritance. Our legacy is the energy we radiate into the universe, touching future generations and feeding the living planet we leave behind. Like the pure waters of Crater Lake reflecting the sky, we mirror back the beauty we absorb, creating a continuous cycle of giving and receiving.

Nature's wisdom speaks in the language of paradox: strength through flexibility, growth through release, creation through destruction. The Washburn fire that had scarred Yosemite's landscape wasn't just destruction—it was renewal. The violent eruption that destroyed Mount Mazama created the serene beauty of Crater Lake. In these paradoxes, I found permission to unmake myself.

We have a tendency to overthink—and complicate—our lives in a search for deep meaning. But what would happen if our sole purpose in life were to experience joy and enhance the conditions that make joy possible for others? I think of Celeste, combining volunteer work with adventure, mixing purpose with play. That's become my mission as I move forward. Nature feeds my joy, and I want to nurture it in return. By embracing these lessons, I'm discovering a new way of being in the world. Like the pure waters of Crater Lake reflecting the sky, I'm learning to mirror back only what's true and essential. This, I believe, is the true gift of this journey—not just the miles covered or the sights seen, but the layers lost along the way, revealing the authentic self that was always there, waiting to emerge.

9.

THE ENERGY OF LIFE

Dates: July 14 – 20
Location: South-Central Oregon
Trails: Rogue River-Siskiyou National Forest (Rogue River Trail), Crater Lake National Park (Garfield Peak, Crater Lake Peak),
Miles Hiked in Week 9: 47.6
Total Miles Hiked: 456.3

SUNDAY MORNING FOUND me battling the overgrown Union Creek trail. After a frustrating half-mile of pushing through encroaching vegetation, I threw in the towel and headed back to the Rogue River trail, lured by a sign for the Natural Bridge. It was the same section I had hiked last week, but I didn't tire of watching the powerful river disappear into an ancient lava tube. Truth be told, I was under the spell of the Rogue River, hiking along its banks, marveling at its many faces—from thunderous rapids to serene pools, from mysterious lava tubes to deep gorges flanked by lush forests.

On Monday morning, I found myself driving into Crater Lake National Park, my sights set on Garfield Peak. My reliable AllTrails app had warned me that the trail might be closed. Now, I'm usually one to follow the rules—closed trails often mean hazardous conditions or protection of wildlife. But this time, reviews suggested a few patches of snow, easily navigable with trekking poles. Armed with my poles and a childhood of Wisconsin snow experience, I bypassed the warning sign. Worst case? I'd turn back. Best case? A spectacular view and a story to tell.

As I encountered my first patch of snow, I easily followed the foot tracks to navigate to the dry trail beyond. A second patch proved equally manageable with help from my poles. When I reached the peak, my breath caught—Crater Lake sprawled before me, its blue waters reaching into the depths of my soul once again. I settled in for some quiet time, savoring my trail mix of cranberries, almonds, and cheese squares as the mountain air carried sweet nature sounds, a symphony just for me. Before heading down, I couldn't resist a playful urge—I made a snowball, placing it at the peak's edge, a little piece of joy left behind.

My solitude was short-lived. Voices approached, and I met a middle-aged couple on the trail. Tourists, by the looks of their clothing. I offered a friendly greeting, but the man launched into a tirade. "Such a stupid sign," he grumbled about the trail closure. Then he shifted gears, complaining about his new RV. "The manual says not to use a garden hose to fill the fresh water tank. How else is a person supposed to fill it? It's the only way!"

I recognized the know-it-all type immediately. Mentioning I was a full-time RVer, I explained about special drinking water hoses. His retort? "I'm a contractor and a hose is a hose." I bit my tongue, wished him luck, and suggested he check Amazon for the difference. I was more than ready to start my descent alone.

But it wasn't the man's demeanor that stuck with me. It was his silent companion. The woman beside him never uttered a word, her eyes downcast, avoiding contact. My years working in domestic violence set off alarm bells. I could almost hear her thoughts: "Whatever I say will be wrong, so I'll just keep quiet." My heart ached, imagining the loneliness she must feel. I found myself hoping she'd find the strength to build a happier life.

As I hiked down, I had to consciously shake off the negative energy from that encounter. Nature, thankfully, provided the perfect antidote. A playful marmot caught my eye, scampering along a branch without a care in the world.

The vast blue sky, glimpses of Crater Lake through the trees, and sparkling snow patches worked their magic, lifting my spirits with each step.

I couldn't help but wonder: How can someone be surrounded by such majesty and still be blind to it? That man had hauled his negativity up a mountain, missing the wonder around him. It was a stark reminder of the energy we create and carry—the kind that draws people in or pushes them away.

Tuesday was a rest day—a "zero" day—but come Wednesday, I was back on the Rogue River trail, tackling the stretch between Woodruff Bridge and Natural Bridge. It was a hiker's dream—beautiful, easy, and I clocked six blissful miles in perfect coherence with the landscape. Knowing I needed to make up for the day before, I repeated the route that evening. Twelve miles in the bag—not too shabby!

Thursday's plan was Diamond Lake, just a stone's throw from Crater Lake National Park. The drive was gorgeous, and I was itching for an easy lakeside bike trail stroll. But as I neared, I saw the familiar sight of smoke from a massive forest fire just north of the lake. Firefighting planes swooped overhead, dousing flames with retardant. My close encounters with wildfires had taught me one thing—distance is your best friend. I quickly turned back, driving to my familiar Rogue River trailhead.

The day took an unexpected turn when I pulled into the parking lot and heard the sickening "crunch" of my Jeep's bumper meeting an unmarked log piling. As I hit the trail, I could feel my energy flagging. The Diamond Lake detour had eaten into my day, and I found myself turning the hike into a chore, focused on clocking miles. Then came the fall—my left foot snagged a tree root, and before I could get my trekking poles in front of me, I was face-first on the ground, like a mighty oak falling in the forest.

I could see the fall in slow motion. My trekking poles, caught in the earth, meant that I had landed solidly with my upper body, my cheek grazing the ground. I laid there, assessing the situation. Legs okay. Arms okay. Maybe a bruise on my cheek. No blood. I took my time standing up, brushing off the leaves and dirt. That's when I noticed I had sprained my thumb while trying to swing my trekking pole forward to catch me. I shook myself off, silently conversing with Celeste, "That was a close call!"

I carried on, gingerly covering the last mile to my Jeep. I had to chuckle—here I was, over 400 miles into my quest. I'd conquered peaks, navigated narrow cliff-side paths, tackled rocky terrain, and even had a rattlesnake encounter. Yet it was this pleasant riverside trail that brought me down. It reminded me of past falls—a Duluth parking lot pothole while I was phone-gazing, a deep rut in Caprock Canyon State Park as I filmed prairie dogs. The common thread? I'd taken my eyes off the path ahead.

I felt lucky, but combined with my earlier bumper incident, a nagging thought crept in—was age catching up with me? But reason quickly kicked in. These were rare mishaps in a life of adventure. Forty years of incident-free driving and far fewer adult injuries than childhood scrapes put things in perspective. Sure, I could hear the concerned voices of friends: "What if you'd hit your head on a rock and passed out?" or "What if you'd been hurt on some isolated part of the trail?" Valid concerns, and I do take precautions—my handy satellite emergency device and sticking to well-marked trails among them. But the fact is, things can change in an instant, no matter how prepared you are.

Here's the thing, though—NOT hiking is a far bigger risk, with guaranteed negative outcomes. A gym session just can't compete with the soul-nourishing power of a nature hike. Giving up solo hiking would be like giving up on life itself. It's that vital to me. The result would be a crushing depression, a darkness hard to shake. So I'll keep hiking as long as these legs will carry me. This quest might be pushing my limits, but it's exactly the challenge I needed at this stage of my life.

As my Oregon adventure neared its end, I couldn't resist one last pilgrimage to Crater Lake National Park on Friday. My target was the 6.4-mile round trip to Crater Peak. The trail didn't disappoint. I scrambled up a rocky hill, then plunged into a forest obstacle course—climbing over, ducking under, and sidestepping fallen trees. But the peak was incredible, a verdant meadow with wildflowers still in bloom. I had this slice of heaven all to myself, and I savored every step of the loop trail, soaking in the panorama of distant forests and mountains.

Following my hike, the day still young, I decided to play tourist on East Rim Drive. The Phantom Shipwreck overlook astounded me; that impossibly blue lake, full of mysteries, tugging at my emotions once again. I played photographer for a pair of older women touring the lake, our brief chat a pleasant interlude. Next stop: the Pinnacles, those eerie spires of volcanic rock standing sentinel over the landscape. Coincidentally, I bumped into the same women again, and we chatted about upcoming adventures. A quick stop at Vidae Falls, and I bid a bittersweet farewell to Crater Lake and its jaw-dropping wonders.

After my wonderful hike, it was time to treat myself to a meal at the local diner, where Friday's special was fish and chips. I nabbed a corner booth, placing my order before the menu even touched the table. It had been an amazing day, and I was glad to sit quietly and observe the interactions taking place in front of me. Diagonally across sat an elderly woman and her middle-aged son, their body language screaming discomfort. Snippets of their conversation drifted over: "She can't disinvite me, I'm the grandma!" They radiated unhappiness, their mood souring further as they nitpicked the waitress's service. I watched, fascinated by how their negativity seemed to feed on itself, growing with each grumble.

Just as my fish and chips arrived, an older couple waltzed in, settling into the booth next to mine. What followed was a comedic dance of musical chairs—first across from each other, then side-by-side facing away, finally landing side-by-side facing me. I couldn't help but chuckle, and when I mentioned it'd make a great short story, the woman's eyes lit up. "Are you a writer too?" she asked.

The question caught me off guard. My mind raced with the usual caveats – "Yes, but I don't make money from it" or "Yes, but it's just a hobby." This time, though, I pushed those thoughts aside. "Yes, I am," I replied simply. And just like that, we were off, diving into a delightful conversation. They shared their story—both widowed, high school alumni reunited. He, it turned out, was a poet. I couldn't help but notice the grumpy mother-son duo had fallen silent, eavesdropping. I wondered if our chat was opening their eyes to life's possibilities.

As I paid my bill, I slipped the waitress some extra cash, making up for the stingy tip that was sure to come her way from the table of complainers. Her shocked gratitude warmed my heart. I left the diner with a new spring in my step, wearing my freshly claimed identity: writer.

Saturday dawned with the promise of adventure—whitewater rafting on the Rogue River. As I drove west, the acrid scent of smoky wildfires filled the air, a reminder of the spreading wildfires and the truth of climate change. Parked at the meeting point, I squeezed in a quick hike on the nearby bike path before our bus arrived, rubber raft in tow.

It didn't take long to reach the launch site, and after a brief lesson, we paddled into the meandering river, with plenty of time to get acquainted before we hit a short stretch of class IV rapids. When asked about home, I shared my full-time RVer status and my 1,000-mile hiking quest. Then came those magic words: "Hey, you should write a book!"

"That's exactly what I'm doing," I replied, the words feeling natural and true. As we approached the rapids, I realized I was embarking on two thrilling journeys—one down this wild river, and another into my new identity as a writer. Both filled me with a sense of excitement and possibility I hadn't felt in years.

Later, tallying my miles for the week, I logged 47.6 miles, a few miles beyond my weekly goal. This felt particularly satisfying given the "zero" day I'd taken. My quest odometer now read 456.3 miles—the 500-mile mark looming tantalizingly close. I'd survived my first fall unscathed, discovered a new identity, and learned that sometimes the most significant transformations happen when we least expect them, on the most ordinary of days.

SUCCESS IS CHOOSING YOUR ENERGY.

Like the Rogue River shifting from thunderous rapids to serene pools, I was learning that we get to choose how we move through the world. When I spoke those words, "I am a writer," they emerged from a spontaneous moment of choosing joy over self-doubt, possibility over limitation. Just as the Rogue River doesn't question which way it should flow, I was learning to trust my natural energy when it felt true and right.

But I also knew that I didn't want to wrap myself in yet another identity based on what I do. Perhaps, to someone I met on the whitewater rafting trip, I was simply "the woman on the raft"—open, engaging, and visibly content with my life. I'm not like that every day, but I can see the magic that happens when I channel my inner Celeste. I draw in fascinating people and conversations without even trying. I become a safe harbor, a lighthouse illuminating life's possibilities.

I have the raw materials to embody that Celeste-like energy. It's not about becoming someone else, but about peeling away the layers to reveal the most authentic version of myself. As I pondered these observations about energy, another postcard arrived from Celeste:

Dear Brenda,

Have you noticed how nature never apologizes for its moods? A thunderstorm doesn't justify its power, a meadow doesn't minimize its gentleness. Each manifestation of energy serves its purpose.

The same force that carves canyons also polishes stones smooth. The difference isn't in the force itself, but in how it's expressed. You're learning to recognize your own force, and to direct it with purpose rather than unconsciously allowing it to be shaped by others' expectations.

Remember: energy flows where attention goes. Choose what you magnify in this world.

Shine on,

Celeste

The natural world offers endless lessons about energy. I thought about that grumbling hiker on Garfield Peak, hauling his negativity up a mountain, missing the majesty around him. How different from last week's couple at Wizard Island, their joy infectious as they played in the snow. We all climb the same mountains, walk the same trails, eat in the same diners—but the energy we bring transforms these shared spaces into entirely different experiences.

I couldn't help but think about mom's life energy—an energy that would soon dim. This week, she had experienced a period of self-pity. I reminded her gently: "Mom, you've had it good for so long. Remember who you are—the woman who learned to swim at 70, the musician who brings smiles to faces, the writer of thoughtful stories, the baker who saved the cemetery with her heart cakes. You rebuilt your life after dad died." Just like that, mom's spirit returned. She was ready for her upcoming surgery. When I offered to help, she insisted, "Stay true to your mission." I realized then that this wasn't just my quest, but mom's too. She was cheering me on from the sidelines of her own battle..

I've come to recognize that energy is contagious. In the diner, I watched how the mother-son duo's complaints created a cloud of tension that affected everyone around them. Their negative energy even reached the waitress, whose service they criticized relentlessly. Yet in that same space, the older couple's playful chair dance and open conversation transformed the atmosphere. Their joy created a bubble of possibility that drew others in—even the complainers fell silent, perhaps glimpsing another way of moving through the world.

The trail offers similar lessons. That silent woman on Garfield Peak had dimmed her light in response to her companion's overbearing energy. I recognized the pattern—how one person's negative force can gradually eclipse another's light. Yet nature itself seemed to reject his complaints about trail signs and RV manuals, the marmot continuing its playful scamper, the lake maintaining its serene blue despite his grumbling presence.

Even my fall on the Rogue River trail taught me something about energy. I had been forcing the hike, turning it into a chore, focusing on logging miles rather than experiencing joy. The trail, in its wisdom, quite literally brought me back to earth. Sometimes we need these moments of forced pause to recognize when we're operating with the wrong energy.

The river itself became my teacher. In one stretch, it thunders through rapids with magnificent force. Around the next bend, it flows silk-smooth and quiet. Through the lava tube at Natural Bridge, it finds an entirely new way of moving. Yet it's all the same water, the same essential nature, just expressing different forms of energy. We humans have this same capacity—to be both gentle and fierce, playful and profound, all while remaining true to our essential nature.

This is what Celeste modeled on the ferry all those years ago. Her energy wasn't about doing or being anything in particular. It was about choosing to remain open to joy, to possibility, to life itself. Whether volunteering on her island or silently watching the sun glint off the water, she maintained that quiet radiance that drew others toward their own light.

As I approach the 500-mile mark of my journey, I'm discovering that the trail offers infinite opportunities to practice choosing our energy. Each mountain peak, each river crossing, each unexpected encounter presents a choice: Will I bring light or shadow? Will I create possibility or limitation? Will I contribute to the world's weight or its wonder?

The answer, I'm learning, lies not in forcing any particular way of being, but in allowing our truest energy to flow, like water finding its natural course. Sometimes that means making snowballs at summit markers. Sometimes it means offering a kind word to a struggling waitress. Sometimes it means simply saying "I am a writer" and letting that truth ripple outward into the world.

10.

THE WEIGHT OF EXPECTATIONS

Dates: July 20 – 26
Location: Central Oregon
Trails: Cove Palisades State Park (Tam-a-lau Trail),
Miles Hiked in Week 10: 49.3
Total Miles Hiked: 505.6

I STARTED WEEK 10 with a final walk to Pearsony Falls, bidding farewell to the Rogue River, Then it was time to head out to my next destination: Cove Palisades State Park. My four-hour drive into the high desert of Oregon went smoothly, but finding my way to the campground turned into a hair-raising adventure.

Spotting a sign for Cove Palisades, I pulled into campground loop E, where I asked for guidance in finding loop C. In return, I received a map and these simple directions: "Your campground is on the other side of the bridge." "No problem," I thought. Leaving the booth, I began my descent towards the marina, the road snaking treacherously between a sheer cliff face and the rushing Deschutes River. Ahead loomed a bridge that seemed to narrow impossibly as I approached. While technically marked for two lanes, I silently thanked whatever road gods were listening that I had it all to myself. I could almost feel the bridge groaning under the weight of my rig, the water far below adding an extra layer of tension to the crossing.

When I finally located my campsite, an audible sigh escaped me. Perched on a hill, the small site would be a tight squeeze for my rig. Driving past, I found a flat area to unhitch the Jeep before looping around the campground to approach my spot at the right angle. With careful maneuvering, I backed into the site and put out my slides, only to discover the Jeep wouldn't fit alongside. Determined, I retracted the slides and inched the rig closer to the electric pedestal, giving me the real estate for the Jeep, and I finished setting up camp.

The sweet relief of hearing the A/C whir to life in the 98-degree heat was short-lived, as Mother Nature decided to throw one last curveball my way—a sudden hail shower. I watched in fascination as pebble-sized ice pellets bounced off my rig, grateful for their brief tenure and lack of damage. The phenomenon of hail on a scorching day never ceases to amaze me, a reminder of nature's capacity for surprise and contrast. It was a rough beginning to the six-night stay ahead.

Once settled, I explored the campground, discovering the trailhead to the Tam-a-láu Trail, its Native American name meaning "place of big rocks on the ground." The trail's moderate rating and 600-foot elevation gain to the canyon rim promised both a challenge and a reward. As I calculated the distance, I realized it was perfect—a loop or two in the campground combined with this trail would satisfy my daily 6.5-mile goal.

However, a quick check of my AllTrails app revealed a bittersweet truth: Tam-a-láu was the only substantial trail in the vicinity. The nearest alternatives were at least an hour's drive away, a prospect made less appealing by the wildfire smoke hanging in the air, diminishing visibility and air quality. Tam-a-láu would be my go-to trail for the week.

The climb to the canyon rim was strenuous, and on that first evening, I greeted an older gentleman, who was on his return trip to the campground. We exchanged greetings and had a short conversation in which he told me that he had recently had a heart stent put in place and he was a cancer survivor. I was impressed, and I congratulated him on his resilience and perseverance.

As the days passed, I often found myself alone on the canyon rim loop, my solitude a stark contrast to the distant hum of motorboats zipping across the river far below. On clear days, the panorama from the rim was remarkable—the snow-capped Cascade Range piercing the horizon, the sinuous paths of the Deschutes and Crooked River canyons carved into the landscape below. From this vantage point, I could trace the wild route that had brought me here, the narrow bridge now looking impossibly small.

Mornings found me tackling the canyon in the cool air, while evenings were reserved for leisurely strolls through the campground, watching the sun's last rays paint the canyon walls in hues of gold and crimson. By midweek, I'll admit, a touch of restlessness had set in. The short duration of my stay at Cove Palisades felt like a blessing, and I found myself eager for new horizons. Then a sobering thought struck me: "What on earth could top Yosemite and Crater Lake?" The possibility that nothing in the coming months would match those experiences was real, and a little daunting.

But I kept hiking, one foot in front of the other, watching the miles accumulate. As Friday approached—day 69 of my journey—I realized I was on the cusp of a significant milestone. The magic number of 500 miles was within reach before Saturday's departure. When I hit that mark, there was no confetti, no cheering crowds. Just me, the trail, and an overwhelming sense of accomplishment. I had reached the halfway point of my quest, and eight days ahead of schedule!

Unable to contain my joy, I broke into an impromptu celebration on the canyon rim. A little dance, a victory song sung to an audience of rocks and sky—it wasn't graceful, but it was genuine. I had pushed my limits, persevered through challenges, and emerged stronger. I gave mom a quick call right there on the rim: "I did it, mom! I just reached 500 miles!" Sharing this milestone with her made the achievement feel complete.

The week's tally filled me with pride: 49.3 miles covered, pushing my total to 505.6 miles. Despite two travel days, I had exceeded my goal, banking an extra 51.1 miles as a buffer for future challenges.

SUCCESS IS RELEASING EXPECTATIONS.

The campground buzzed with life each evening as I made my rounds—children weaving on bikes, families gathering at picnic tables, and laughter drifting between sites. These scenes of togetherness kept drawing my thoughts to my own child, who had recently found work after spending ten months in a homeless shelter. The path that led him there was complicated, marked by choices and circumstances too complex to untangle. During those dark months, he had withdrawn, only recently allowing me back into his orbit as he rebuilt his life.

My journey into motherhood was unconventional from the start. I chose to become a single mother, adopting a little girl from Ukraine just before her seventh birthday. As that child approached adulthood, she identified as male, and I've stood by him through every subsequent name change, determined to offer unwavering support. But I have to admit, I burdened him with expectations—college, career, financial prosperity, happiness. In my mind, that equation equaled "success" for him.

The reality, of course, is far more nuanced. His path is uniquely his own, shaped by early traumatic experiences that I can empathize with but never fully understand. Looking back, I can feel the turbulence that has characterized our relationship. There's a painful truth I've had to confront: to save myself, I had to "push" him out of my house at age 20.

Those days are etched in my memory, vivid and painful. I can still feel the knot in my stomach as I'd detour to the tavern on my way home, grabbing a drink or two before facing the dark energy that seemed to envelop our house. The air would be thick with tension, punctuated by verbal skirmishes over household chores and yard work. I'd established rules in a desperate attempt to maintain order, but they only seemed to deepen the divide between us. Then came that night—the night my son pushed me, and I realized with a sickening clarity that I could no longer defend myself against him. I became fearful of my own child.

Recognizing that higher education wasn't in his plans and minimum wage jobs were his likely future, I helped him land a position at the Grand Canyon, with employer-provided housing. For over five years, he maintained this job, a period of relative stability that brought me immense relief. But old habits die hard, and his struggles with tidiness eventually cost him his housing and, consequently, his job. When he was evicted last year, I abruptly halted my travels, rushing to Arizona to help him chart a new course. The idea of him living with me in the RV was untenable, and the level of support he required far exceeded what I could offer.

His newfound stability became a catalyst for my own transformation. As I watched him rebuild his life, it sparked an epiphany: if I truly want to embody the spirit of acceptance and unconditional love, I need to release my grip on expectations entirely. As a society, we toss around the concepts of "winners" and "losers," often using wealth and job titles to sort people into categories. What we don't admit is that we don't start on an even playing field. A child raised in a loving family in a safe community with financial resources has advantages that someone like my child, who started his early life malnourished and raised in an impoverished violent family, will never have.

As I pondered these realizations about expectations and acceptance, another postcard arrived from Celeste:

Dear Brenda,

The most beautiful gardens aren't those where every plant grows according to plan, but where each is allowed to find its own shape, its own season, its own way of reaching toward the light.

Your son's journey may not match the path you envisioned, but it's authentically his. Just as no one could have prescribed your winding road to joy, his route will unfold according to lessons only he can learn, in timing only his soul understands.

The strongest roots grow not from our expectations, but from knowing we're loved exactly as we are. Your acceptance of his unique journey is perhaps the greatest gift you can offer—the freedom to become himself without the weight of proving his worth.

With compassionate understanding,

Celeste

I treasured Celeste's postcard, but I craved more. I wanted the "how." But she remained silent on this front. Perhaps this was her way of teaching me that there is no formula for unconditional love—it comes from releasing our grip on outcomes, from trusting that each person must find their own way. My son's path wouldn't be found in my careful plans or earnest hopes, but in his own steps forward, however uncertain they might seem. The "how" was simply to let go.

As I hiked the familiar canyon rim trail, my mind wandered to the origins of my backpack—those expectations I carry with me. I realized that many of these burdens weren't given to me by my parents. They were high school graduates who simply expected us to work hard and take responsibility for our lives. They never pushed me towards college or grad school, never judged me as a "loser" when I hit rock bottom. Their faith in me never wavered. No, I was the one who had lost faith in myself. I am still my own harshest critic, shouldering expectations that no one else places on me.

If my parents could love unconditionally, without expectations, then so can I. And with perfect timing, my son called, excitedly sharing his plans for treating me for dinner when I see him over the Christmas holiday. I could hear the pride in his voice. No matter how painful the experience, he had come out the other side with a stronger sense of agency and gratitude. He was in a safe place, making friends, and unlike his first time at the Grand Canyon, sending me photos of sunsets. I was proud of him—not for meeting any external measure of success, but for finding his way forward on his own terms.

On Saturday morning, I hitched up my Jeep and headed north. An eight-hour drive lay ahead, but my heart felt lighter than it had in months. As I drove from the arid Oregon high desert to the lush greens of Washington's Olympic Peninsula, I reflected on my own transformation. With 500 miles under my hiking boots, I felt ready for whatever challenges and joys awaited me.

11.

THE EDGE

Dates: July 28 – August 3
Location: Olympic Peninsula, Washington
Trails: Anderson Lake State Park, Fort Flagler Historical State Park, HJ Carroll County Park, Fort Worden Historical State Park (Bluff Loop), Larry Scott Trail
Miles Hiked in Week 11: 44.2
Total Miles Hiked: 549.8

I WOKE UP Sunday morning with the realization that this was going to be "home" for the next 30 days. While excited to explore the area and get a reprieve from the heat, I also recognized my own patterns. My love for change and curiosity often drive me forward, sometimes to my limits. This desire for novelty is a double-edged sword, keeping life exciting but potentially leading to restlessness. Would boredom take over? Or could I reconcile the tension between my need to decelerate and my spirit's craving for movement?

Perhaps the answer lay not in choosing between adventure and rootedness, but in finding adventure within rootedness. Could I approach each day in this familiar setting with the same curiosity and openness I bring to new destinations? Could I train my eyes to see the extraordinary in the ordinary, to find novelty in routine?

My test soon began, as the morning greeted me with what I learned was typical weather: overcast, grey, chilly, and downright gloomy. As I set out to find my go-to trail, the kind I could return to day after day for some easy and interesting miles, I found myself struggling against an unexpected enemy—the closed-in atmosphere of the dense forests.

My first venture to Anderson Lake State Park set the tone. Warning signs kept visitors away from the algae-infested lake, and as I started down the trail, I found myself in a fern-covered forest so thick it seemed to swallow daylight. I felt . . . off. A sense of claustrophobia crept over me, an unsettling feeling I hadn't experienced in ages. Even photographing the countless foot bridges— usually a joy—felt like a chore.

I woke up Monday feeling tired, with dark clouds and intermittent rain marking my day. It was a good day to take care of some errands, including visiting a local cat hotel, where Coco and Izzy would be staying while I'm in Canada next week. It had been years since I needed a cat sitter or had to board the cats, and I was anxious about leaving them for an entire week. But I wanted the freedom of driving into Canada in my Jeep and staying at a friend's place on Gabriola Island. After a couple of visits to the vet to get the cats up to date on their vaccinations, their space in the Cat Hotel was secured.

On Tuesday, I awoke to more gloomy weather. I could feel the gray weather dimming my enthusiasm for hiking and writing. Still, I drove to Fort Flagler State Park and set out on a trail that eventually meandered through historical features. I stopped at the museum to learn more about the fort, established in 1897 to protect Puget Sound from enemy ships and planes that never arrived.

Again, the dark clouds and thick forests turned hiking into a chore. For the third day in a row, I wasn't enjoying my hikes. I began to wonder if this heavy, cloudy feeling amidst the dense woods would be with me for my entire stay in Washington. On my return, I stopped at Mystery Bay State Park, which was nothing more than a parking loop with a boat launch. A red boat bobbing in the water broke up the grayness of the day. Despite my mood, I ended the day with a little over six miles.

Wednesday was a blissfully sunny day. I returned to Port Townsend for a walk, an ice cream treat, and a little shopping. I could feel my mood lift and my energy return. I didn't have a set destination for my walk, and I was several miles short of my goal when I returned to the RV park. I had noticed a sign for a small county park—HJ Carroll Park—just a mile away, so I checked out the short loop that circumnavigated the park. I was pleasantly surprised to discover a small trail down to Chimacum Creek built by the local Scout group, and a wide trail that wound alongside a farm. The trail was the inspiration of a local resident who believed trails should extend to local schools, neighborhoods, businesses, and gathering places. I left inspired and glad to have found a local trail that would help me reach my mileage goals.

I had been feeling out of sync this week, as if my spirit was lagging. But then came Thursday's discovery of Fort Worden Historical State Park's Bluff Trail. From the Point Wilson lighthouse to North Beach, from marshlands to stunning overlooks, the trail was a feast for the senses. A chance encounter with a sea otter rolling in the sand felt like nature's way of welcoming me back to the joy of discovery

As I came to an area known as the Chinese Gardens, I stopped to read this sign:

Life on the Edge

Forests, wetlands, farmlands and ocean shoreline are distinct landscape communities or habitats. These four different habitats come together here at Chinese Gardens.

Wildlife and plants from each community mix together in the edges where these landscapes meet. Together, they form a unique blended neighborhood with greater numbers and variety of species. Animals, birds and vegetation each benefit from overlapping habitats. This is known as the "edge effect."

As I continued up the trail, the views were incredible. Leaning over the railing at the old Searchlight Station, I took in a deep breath of ocean air, the salty tang mixing with the earthy scent of the nearby forest. The abandoned military structures added an eerie atmosphere, secrets and spirits seemed to lurk in the shadows. The overlook offered a picture-perfect view of the lighthouse, and a chance encounter with a friendly couple led me to the inspiring Memories Vault—a sculpture garden featuring poems by local poet Sam Hamill. I had found the trail that spoke to my heart and would put a smile back on my face.

It was a fantastic adventure, and after a quick visit to the vet, I returned to HJ Carroll Park to add a few miles before the sun went down. As I walked the memorial path intersecting a farm, I found myself wondering if the trail continued beyond the T-intersection ahead. Two women approached, each walking a dog. I seized the opportunity to ask about the trail's end. They were friendly enough, explaining there wasn't much to see beyond the turn-around point. I was about to thank them and move on when suddenly—WHAM! One of the dogs lunged at me, catching everyone off guard. I stumbled towards the fence line, and that's when I noticed blood trickling down my arm. The dog had actually bitten me!

The owner was mortified. She introduced the dog as Bella, explaining she'd recently "inherited" her after a friend—the dog's original owner—had passed away. The name Bella struck me as an odd coincidence, given that my cat's name is Isabella. As the owner assured me about Bella's up-to-date rabies vaccine, she offered her contact information in case I needed medical attention. And that's when the twilight zone moment hit—her name was CELESTE!

I mean, what are the odds? Celeste's dog bit me! I couldn't help but wonder if there was some deeper meaning to this bizarre coincidence. Or was it just that—a wild, meaningless coincidence?

Back at the RV, I discovered a deep puncture wound where the dog's tooth had pierced my skin. After a quick consult with my dog-loving sister-in-law, I made a pharmacy run for antibiotic cream and a larger bandage. I cleaned the wound meticulously, keeping a watchful eye for any signs of infection and researching local Urgent Care options, just in case.

On Friday morning, I put a fresh bandage on my wound, and drove into Port Townsend, where I walked to the boat haven and connected with the Larry Scott Trail, which paralleled the water toward the papermill. I cut my walk short, returning to downtown, where I hopped aboard the Admiral Jack, a touring vessel, for a jaunt around the bay. The salty spray and exhilarating ride were a welcome break from the trails. After my rocky start, I was finally warming up to the local trails. The key, I realized, was to seek out trails with open vistas to combat the darkness of the deep mossy forests.

Saturday's outing included a trip to the farmer's market to pick up sourdough bread, and a quick hike on Fort Worden's Bluff Loop trail. But my mind was preoccupied with my upcoming trip to British Columbia. Late afternoon, I took Coco and Isabella to the cat hotel. Was it possible to feel more anxious dropping my cats off at the hotel than I did dropping my child off for the first day of school? I packed my suitcase for the week and loaded up my Jeep, preparing for an early morning to catch the 6:20 ferry out of Port Townsend.

What a peculiar week this turned out to be! Despite my best efforts, I couldn't quite make up for that sluggish Monday, falling short of my weekly goal by 1.3 miles. I clocked in at 44.2 miles, bringing my grand total to 549.8 miles.

That sign about "Life on the Edge" kept resonating in my mind all week long. Here I was, deep in the middle of this 1,000-mile quest, feeling like I was walking in my own transition zone. I was slowly learning this new terrain. The dense forests had initially felt oppressive, but by seeking trails that balanced forest and shore, I was finding my way. Perhaps that was the key to this entire journey—not avoiding the edges, but learning to thrive there.

SUCCESS IS FINDING COURAGE TO THRIVE AT LIFE'S BOUNDARIES.

Reflecting on my hikes, I found myself captivated by these boundaries—where forest meets shore, where civilization meets wilderness, where comfort meets challenge. Each trail offered its own lesson in navigating these transitions. The Bluff Trail at Fort Worden, with its mix of dense forest opening suddenly to breathtaking ocean views, became a metaphor for my journey. Sometimes we have to push through the darkness to find the light.

I was in a place of uncertainty—with my health and my future. Would I be okay after the dog bite? And what did I want for my future? I had started the week feeling out of sorts, and I ended the week feeling almost lost, as if life were just one big question mark.

As another postcard from my friend Celeste arrived, her words seemed to illuminate my muddled thoughts:

Dear Brenda,

Funny how life keeps shoving us to the edges, isn't it? Boundaries, thresholds— whatever you call them—they can be downright uncomfortable. But that's where transformation happens.

Think about those trails you've hiked. The best views came when the trees thinned out, when the land shifted. That's no accident. Growth happens where habitats meet. And so it is with us—we grow most at the edges of our comfort zones.

Even that unexpected bite came at a crossroads, where your path intersected with my namesake. Life has a way of nudging us forward with its little surprises, doesn't it?

The tidepools at the edge of the ocean hold more diversity than either land or sea alone. You're learning to thrive in these in-between spaces.

Keep walking. Trust the trail.

Sending courage,

Celeste

My daily walks through the RV co-op resort were revealing a possible future I hadn't considered. Some residents lived in lovely park models rather than RVs—modern "tiny houses," each about 400 square feet with porches and decks. Who would've thought? Me, the full-time RVer, suddenly afflicted with "tiny house envy."

The truth is, I know there will come a day when I'll tire of driving my big motorhome. Travel will always be my lifeblood, but the shape of it might evolve. I could picture myself in one of these tiny houses, with a nimble camper van ready to whisk me away on new adventures at a moment's notice. The future is a blank canvas, and I'm not sure where I'll find my "home" or what kind of community will embrace me.

Life's boundaries took on deeper meaning as mom underwent her mastectomy surgery. The transition from health to disease, from vitality to vulnerability—with countless gradations in between—became starkly real. When I called to check in, her voice sounded tired and cracked, yet the news was encouraging: the surgery had gone well, and she had entered the recovery stage.

During our conversation, she steered the talk toward my adventures, finding in my stories a brief escape from her medical reality. Even from her bed, mom maintained her remarkable positivity, already speaking of plans to return to her active lifestyle. I took comfort knowing my sister would be staying with her for the next three weeks, providing the daily care and companionship mom needed during this critical recovery period. In her resilience, I glimpsed another boundary being navigated—between accepting present limitations and holding onto future possibilities.

Life, I've come to realize, is an intricate spiderweb, each strand carefully spun and interconnected. A single thread might seem insignificant on its own, but together, they form something powerful and purposeful. The dog bite incident, the gloomy forests, the surprising desire for a more permanent home—they're all threads in this web I'm weaving.

Despite attempts to stay present, my mind wandered to the future—planning next week's adventure, pondering what "home" might look like as I age. But I pulled myself back by recalling three vivid scenes from the week: that breathtaking view of Point Wilson lighthouse from Bluff Trail; the playful otter that swam ashore, frolicking in the sand just yards away; and the exhilarating feel of wind in my hair and misty spray on my face aboard the tour boat. These moments, brimming with awe and wonder, are what make life rich and vibrant.

As I prepare for Canada, I realize that each unexpected encounter—whether it's a dog bite or a moment of clarity on a misty trail has pushed me further along my path. I'm learning that life's richest moments often come when we stand at the edge, gathering our courage to take the next step forward.

12.

THE PASSENGER SEAT

Dates: August 4 – 10
Location: British Columbia, Canada
Trails: Gabriola Island (community trails, Pilot Bay and Taylor Bay trails, Fin Norwich Seagirt Waterfront, Brickyard Beach, Elder Cedar Trail), Salt Spring Island (Ruckle Provincial Park)
Miles Hiked in Week 12: 51.1
Total Miles Hiked: 600.9

DAWN BROKE OVER Port Townsend as I joined the line of vehicles waiting for the 6:30 ferry. Steam rose from my travel mug of Earl Grey tea as I watched the sun pierce through stubborn clouds, painting the sky in soft rose and amber. For once, I wasn't behind the wheel of my RV, managing every detail. Today, I would be the woman on the ferry—a passenger surrendering to the journey ahead. The irony wasn't lost on me; after all these months of seeking to embody Celeste's spirit, here I was, literally following her path across the water.

The trip to British Columbia had been months in the making, born from an invitation to visit a friend on Gabriola Island. Planning proved challenging—coordinating schedules across time zones, navigating ferry schedules, and working around summer tourist season. My usual approach of planning ahead and booking tours didn't work in this setting.

By the time we finally locked in a date, it was too late to snag a reservation on the ferry from Port Angeles. After some back-and-forth, we cobbled together a new plan: I'd take the ferry from Port Townsend, swing by the Vancouver airport to pick up my friend, and then we'd island-hop via a couple more ferries to reach our final destination—Gabriola Island, part of the Southern Gulf Islands in the Strait of Georgia.

This trip marked another new experience I'd have to navigate—for the first time in my RV life I'd be leaving Coco and Izzy behind. The cat hotel I found seemed perfect, with its playground and big windows for bird-watching, and I knew the cats would be fine. But being on my own for so long, I've grown accustomed to being the captain of my ship. For the week, I'd have to learn to relax and embrace the passenger seat.

Once aboard the Port Townsend ferry, I made the most of the 35-minute crossing, pacing the upper deck to log some steps while catching glimpses of the mist-enshrouded island. The ferry brought me to Whidbey Island, where I drove through a tapestry of small towns, dense forests, sprawling meadows, and breathtaking shorelines. The drive over Deception Pass bridge was particularly spectacular—a reminder of why I love exploring the backroads. The relaxing journey continued all the way to I-5, my mind relishing the lush landscape at every turn.

At the Canadian border, I flashed my passport and switched my focus to the unfamiliar kilometer readings on my dashboard. Perfect timing brought me to the Vancouver airport just as my friend, "Jenn," emerged from baggage claim. We'd been virtual accountability buddies since meeting through a business coach years ago, but this was our first face-to-face encounter. We laughed and hugged at finally meeting in person.

With time to spare, we explored Granville Island's public markets, grabbing a bite before hopping on a cheerful little blue boat for a tour of Vancouver's impressive skyline. Jenn and I caught up on family happenings, business, and life, bridging the gap between our online relationship and this new, tangible friendship.

The afternoon found us boarding a behemoth of a ferry at Tsawwassen terminal—a vessel so massive it could have passed for a cruise ship. Marveling at its vehicle capacity, we made note of our car's location before heading to the upper deck. While Jenn basked in the sunshine, I added to my step count, circling the deck throughout the two-hour journey to Nanaimo on Vancouver Island. The trip's highlight? A humpback whale breaching in the distant waters, eliciting gasps of awe from fellow passengers.

Our island-hopping adventure concluded with a final ferry to Gabriola Island, where we met our hosts, "Connie" and "Bill." Connie, a long-time friend of Jenn's from their Yukon days, immediately struck me as a kindred spirit with her no-nonsense attitude. Amusingly, both Connie and Jenn bemoaned the "heat wave"—temperatures in the 70s Fahrenheit that felt positively refreshing to me after months of scorching weather. Their discomfort was my relief.

As evening fell, I retreated to my own slice of paradise—their motorhome, thoughtfully parked in the front yard for my use. I looked at the day's mileage, pleased with the 6.1 miles I had walked while ferrying across the various bodies of water. Yet as I settled in for the night, I recognized that this week would be about more than just logging miles. My physical journey was about to take a backseat to something deeper—a lesson in letting go.

For the first time in ages, I slept in! No cats pawing me awake, no carefully crafted schedule demanding my attention. The simple act of surrendering to sleep revealed how tightly I'd been gripping the reins of my daily life. Just pure, unadulterated rest.

I've often quipped, "My life is a vacation," given my nomadic lifestyle of crisscrossing the country, soaking in breathtaking sights, and collecting unforgettable experiences—all while trying to cobble together a living. But as the days unfolded, I realized just how bone-deep tired I was. Surprisingly, it wasn't the physical toll of hiking that had worn me down; it was the constant mental gymnastics of decision-making that comes with solo living.

Being on my own means shouldering every single decision, every single day. I'm the CEO, CFO, and sole employee of my life enterprise. While I had initially chafed at the delays in planning this trip, now that I was here, I felt ready to loosen my grip on the reins. I distilled my goals for the week down to two essentials: meet my hiking mileage target and go on a whale watching adventure. Everything else? I decided to leave it to serendipity.

I began Monday morning with a solo walk on the gravel road, eventually ducking into the local community park. There I found myself winding through one of the many wooded trails on the island. Its close proximity would make it an easy go-to trail for the week. And then, it was time to slip into the passenger seat, both literally and figuratively. With Connie at the wheel, our first stop was the beach, where we waded into the water at low tide. Jenn and I returned at sunset, only to discover the beach had pulled a disappearing act at high tide.

On Tuesday, I looked at the map of Gabriola Island, discovering that it was dotted with community parks, each featuring well-marked trails that weave through different parts of the island. I found the trailhead to the 707 Community Park, and as I strolled along these trails, I couldn't help but smile at the whimsical touches left by residents—dreamcatchers hanging from trees, solar lanterns lighting the way, gnomes peeking from behind rocks, and even charming little farm stands. My walks were a delightful mix of roads, trails, and seashores, which kept me entertained throughout the day. I pushed myself to cover some extra miles, and in doing so, satisfied my curiosity with the question of what lay beyond that last hill.

A rhythm began to take form for the week. Solo hikes, group walks, outings to the market, a few events, and dinner together. On Wednesday, the three of us found ourselves rock jumping at low tide. While my treks in the community parks were interesting, nothing compared to the playful walks along the sea. We leaped from rock to rock, occasionally spotting a harbor seal bobbing in the water, breathing in the salty sea air, climbing over bleached logs, and examining the odd crevices in the rocks. We ended the evening at the nearby Brickyard Beach, listening to live bands as the sun dipped below the horizon. It was a fantastic day, with plenty of miles and shared laughs.

Thursday arrived, and I was beyond excited by the afternoon's adventure— a whale watching tour! I began the morning with a solo walk along the shore, and then prepped for our ferry ride to Nanaimo, where we checked in and suited up in our red floater coveralls. I couldn't help but laugh as we looked like red walruses, strutting down the gangway to climb into the 12-passenger Zodiac. I was all smiles as we zoomed off in search of whales in the corridors of the Gulf Islands.

What happened next shattered every expectation I had about encounters with nature. We had stopped to watch some whales in the distance, when our captain received word of another whale nearby. We zoomed over, stopping near two other boats, where we met Wisp, a humpback whale who would teach me the most profound lesson about surrendering control. While regulations required boats to maintain a 100-meter distance from marine wildlife, Wisp had her own agenda. As our captain cut the engine, I felt the familiar urge to reach for my camera, to document and control the moment. But something made me pause.

Wisp's enormous body glided closer, until she was mere feet from our Zodiac. The sound of her exhalation through her blowhole broke the silence, a powerful whoosh that seemed to vibrate through the air and into our bones. Time seemed to stop as her eye met mine—an ancient intelligence regarding our Zodiac with gentle curiosity. In that moment, I knew who was in charge of this adventure. Here was a creature who could easily overturn our boat with a flick of her massive tail, yet she moved with incredible grace and intention. My heart pounded as she slipped beneath our Zodiac, emerging on the other side with balletic precision.

Wisp flirted with our fleet of boats for at least 20 minutes. She swam back and forth, dipping under the vast ocean waters before surfacing with a playful grin on her massive face. That final wave of her fluke felt like a benediction— a reminder that some of life's most extraordinary moments come not when we're gripping the wheel tightly, but when we're willing to sit back in awe and simply receive what the universe offers.

As the week progressed, Jenn and I decided to give Connie and Bill a break from their roles as hosts. They had fed us, guided us, and accompanied us, and we didn't want to impose on their hospitality. So on Friday, Jenn and I took the ferry to Vancouver Island, drove south, and then boarded the ferry to Salt Spring Island, known for its vibrant artist community and galleries. We strolled through town, wandered along the beach, and enjoyed a seashore walk in Ruckle Provincial Park.

Saturday marked my last full day on Gabriola Island. We started the day at the Saturday market, then marveled at an enormous cedar tree on the Elder Cedar Trail, and finally spent some time soaking up the sun on the beach. We enjoyed our final meal together, and I packed up for my early morning drive to the ferry dock. I was satisfied that I had reached both of my physical goals for the week, claiming 51.1 miles. Incredibly, I had reached my 600-mile mark. I was on the backend of my 1,000-mile quest.

As I've been reminded week after week, this journey is only part physical. And this week, my physical journey took a backseat to the emotional, psychological, and mental components of my quest. "Control" became the central theme, and I became hyper-alert of how each of us, including myself, exerts our own habits, peculiarities, and pace into relationships with others. As the week unfolded, I found myself reflecting on deeper questions of connection, independence, and the shape of my life.

SUCCESS LIES IN SURRENDERING CONTROL.

Long before I stepped on the ferry, I felt frustrated. I had to wait on others to finalize their plans, and the delay meant that all the reservations on the direct ferry to Gabriola Island were taken. I had to make alternate travel plans. My schedule was at the mercy of others. Once the new plan was in place, I let out a sigh of relief.

It turns out, that introduction to "playing with people" was just the beginning of what sometimes turned into a contentious week. Traveling with Jenn tested my patience, highlighting the differences in our approaches to time and consideration. Our contrasting styles—my efficiency versus her leisurely pace—created moments of tension that forced me to examine my own rigidity and need for control.

By Friday, my patience had worn thin. After yet another unannounced "detour" by Jenn, I found myself turning back, frustration bubbling over. "Goddammit, Jenn," I called out, finally voicing my irritation. I explained how her constant, unplanned stops felt like a form of control, and how it was especially concerning given the lack of cell service on the island. I asked Jenn to just let me know when she wanted to stop and look. I was happy to oblige, but this disappearing act that left me standing on the street alone was not my idea of fun.

And then there was Connie, who wanted our help in the kitchen, but insisted that everything be done just right. I found myself straddling the line between helping and incurring her wrath should an item be stored in the wrong place. It felt like a lose-lose situation. All three of us had brought our own choreography to this improvised dance—Jenn with her meandering pace and spontaneous detours, Connie with her precise kitchen protocols, and me with my carefully measured miles and timetables. Each of us, in our own way, was trying to conduct the symphony of our shared days. The friction between our styles wasn't just about control; it was about learning to harmonize our different rhythms.

As I studied my own emotional reactions, deeper questions emerged about relationships, solitude, and connection. I found myself pondering my journey of self-discovery—the years of poverty, single motherhood, and the careful construction of my independent life. Since RV life, I've accepted the mysteries of the universe, and flowed with the rhythm of the seasons. But this week showed me that I need to do some work while sitting in the passenger seat of life. Can I let go and enjoy the surprises that come my way?

A postcard from my friend Celeste arrived, as if sensing my introspective mood:

Dear Brenda,

Isn't it fascinating how the passenger seat offers a completely different view of the journey? From behind the wheel, we focus on the destination, the route, the next turn.

But when we surrender control, we notice things we've been missing—the way sunlight dapples through trees, the subtle shifts in the landscape, the quiet moments between breaths.

These friends of yours—each with their own way of moving through the world—they're teachers too. Sometimes the greatest lessons come through the friction of different rhythms finding their way to dance together.

Let yourself be carried by the current of life sometimes. The view is extraordinary from here.

Here's to the unplanned magic,

Celeste

On Saturday, we enjoyed our final meal together. That's when Bill expressed concern over the wound from last week's dog bite. As Connie brought out antibacterial silver mesh and dressed my wound with care, the universe's message became clearer. The bite was a vivid reminder that no matter how carefully we plan, life has its own way of breaking through our defenses. I began to realize that maybe the message was about control. We plan, organize, and scheme to minimize risk and improve the odds of enjoying a great experience.

But in the end, we don't have control of our fate. Despite our best intentions, bad things happen. Would I be okay? I wasn't so confident as I packed my bags for my early morning departure.

Meanwhile, mom was learning her own lessons about control. A post-surgery appointment revealed that the cancer had spread further than initially thought. Chemotherapy and radiation might prolong her life, but she would have to endure the harsh treatments. After careful consideration, she chose quality over quantity—ready to let the disease progress to its natural conclusion rather than fight a battle that would diminish her remaining days. The news left me shaken, but I was proud of her clarity. She made the choice that best suited her spirit. While she couldn't control the outcome, she could influence the process and how she lived her remaining time.

And maybe Wisp's message was the same. We headed out in Zodiacs, with the expectation we would see whales. But to be "mugged" by a humpback whale? That was beyond my wildest dreams. The image that will stay with me forever is the bobbing head of Wisp, our shared eye contact, and the enormity of her power. She was in full control of the seas, and we had to surrender to her as she swam beneath our Zodiac. It was an exciting thrill that could have ended disastrously. And maybe that's the lesson? Sometimes, we have to ride in the passenger seat, and some of our biggest thrills will be unplanned, unexpected, and amazing.

As the week ended, I was proud, having crossed the 600-mile mark on my hiking quest. But as I packed the extra medical supplies, I knew I had to be ready to seek urgent care should my wound become worse. And as I considered the miles ahead of me, I felt more excited than fearful.

In many ways, every step of this quest was about letting go of control, and recognizing that nature and happenstance will determine my ultimate success. And if something beyond my control derails my quest? The old me would have seen that as failure. But after dancing with Wisp beneath the Canadian sky, after surrendering to the ebb and flow of island time, I understand differently now. Success isn't about maintaining perfect control—it's about staying open to the magic that happens when we let go. Whatever lies ahead in these final 400 miles, I know I've already succeeded in the most important way: I've learned to trust the journey.

13.

THE SHADOW VALLEY

Dates: August 11 – 17
Location: Olympic Peninsula, Washington
Trails: Fort Worden Historical State Park (Bluff Loop), Olympic National Park (Lake Angeles Trail), Miller Peninsula State Park
Miles Hiked in Week 13: 45.8
Total Miles Hiked: 646.7

WEEK 13 OF MY 1,000-mile quest unfolded beneath a twilight of shadows in the early morning sky. I rose early, hugged my friends goodbye, and boarded the 6:20 ferry to Vancouver Island. As we left the dock, I stood at the railing, marveling at the rising sun casting an orange tint on the outlying islands. From the ferry landing, I made a beeline south to Victoria, known as the "Garden City" for its colorful gardens, parks, and blooms. Without a reservation in hand, I was glad to check in early, receiving the lucky number thirteen—that's where I stood in the standby line, odds in my favor for the 10:30 crossing.

With a long wait ahead of me, and bound by border regulations to stay on the dock, I transformed this limbo into opportunity. I paced the length of the docking area, clocking easy miles while other passengers waited in their vehicles. A father leading his two young sons in a pushup challenge caught my eye—at least I wasn't the only one turning waiting into workout time.

When my Jeep finally squeezed onto the ferry, I made my way to the upper deck, determined to make this crossing count. Each loop brought me to the bow, where I leaned into a strong headwind, its bite sharp against my face. There was something exhilarating about this dance with the elements, surrounded by the vast expanse of ocean. As we neared Port Angeles, a fellow passenger approached, curious about my loops on the deck. Checking my app, I proudly announced my seven-mile accomplishment. It felt good to start the day with such energy, a physical manifestation of my eagerness to return home.

Back on American soil, I made the hour-long drive to the RV and then rushed to my most anticipated reunion—picking up Coco and Isabella from the cat hotel. Their chorus of meows filled the car, a symphony that brought a smile to my face. But something shifted as I drove through the perpetual gray of the Olympic Peninsula. The energy that had carried me across the morning's ferry crossing ebbed away, replaced by an inexplicable heaviness. Even reuniting with my cats and returning to my own space couldn't shake this creeping melancholy

Perhaps it was the news about mom, or the dog bite wound that cast me into this funk. Mom's future had taken on a painful clarity. Mine, however, remained uncertain. Once home, I carefully cleaned the wound and applied a fresh dressing, knowing I would need to monitor it closely in the days ahead. It was a small but persistent worry hovering in the back of my mind—a physical reminder of how vulnerable we all are, even in our strongest moments. The parallel between my minor injury and mom's major battle wasn't lost on me, though the scales were vastly different.

Monday dawned beneath a blanket of gray skies, and the week would be punctuated by sporadic rain showers that seemed to mirror my waning enthusiasm. In hopes of lifting my spirits, I returned to Fort Worden, meandering through the park, stumbling upon new trails and learning more about the "Chinese gardens," a once-thriving vegetable garden now transformed into a lagoon and marshland. I detoured to the beach, soaking in the soothing sound of waves gently splashing against the shore. But even this moment of tranquility couldn't shake my downtrodden mood.

My walks felt forced, each mile a chore. On Tuesday, I walked around Port Townsend, ducking in shops and splurging on a new fleece jacket. But I was worn out, and returned to the RV to nap. In the evening, I was back at the county park, hoping I wouldn't run into Celeste's dog a second time.

Wednesday marked rock bottom. The heaviness I'd been fighting finally won, sending me back to bed after merely feeding the cats. The irony wasn't lost on me—my wound was healing nicely, my mileage goals were within reach, yet here I was, unable to move. Logging just 2.4 miles that day forced me to confront an uncomfortable truth: this wasn't about physical fatigue. Something deeper was at work.

I knew that time was running out for mom. After researching options, I booked a flight to Minneapolis for November. From there, a friend would drive me to the farm. I would spend ten days with mom over the Thanksgiving holiday. Ten days to tell her I loved her. Ten days to say goodbye. The decision brought both sorrow and relief—a path forward through the emotional fog that had enveloped me.

Thursday dawned with a glimmer of hope as the sun finally pierced the cloud cover, casting long shadows across the landscape. Seizing this rare brightness, I set out early for Olympic National Park, my sights set on Lake Angeles. Upon arriving at the trailhead, I was greeted by a large orange sign:

COUGAR FREQUENTING AREA
BE ALERT
SOLO HIKING NOT ADVISED.

The month-old warning stirred a primal fear, yet somehow felt fitting. Just as a cougar might be lurking in these woods, my own shadows were stalking my thoughts. I stood there, weighing my options: turn back and seek a different trail, abandon the challenge entirely, or face whatever waited on the trail—both the physical dangers and the emotional ones. The nearly full parking lot offered some solace that I would have company on the trail, but the deeper fears? Those I would have to face alone.

The dense forest closed in around me as I started up the trail, the smell of damp earth filling my nostrils. Each crackle of a twig sent my heart racing, but I pressed on, one vigilant step at a time. Gradually, the beauty of my surroundings pushed thoughts of lurking cougars to the back of my mind. The 3.7-mile ascent, while challenging, revealed an interesting quirk of Washington trails—their difficulty ratings seemed consistently overstated. What AllTrails labeled as "hard," I would have classified as "moderate."

The lake, when I reached it, presented its own challenges. I scrambled over fallen trees and through thick underbrush, searching for the perfect photo opportunity. And something else felt "off" about the day's hike. The hikers I passed seemed as reserved as the landscape—no friendly hellos or trail chat, just quick nods and averted eyes. How different from the easy camaraderie I'd found on California and Oregon trails. Yet even in this muted atmosphere, small wonders emerged—the way sunlight filtered through evergreen branches, the soft percussion of my boots on pine needles, the unexpected grace of a bird swooping between trees.

Friday drew me to Miller Peninsula State Park, where a narrow trail led to a secluded beach. Bull kelp lay in tangled heaps along the shore, their stems stretching an impressive ten feet or more. The ocean vistas made the frequent consultations with my AllTrails app worthwhile, though even the crash of waves against the shore felt muted, as if playing through a thick fog.

Saturday offered a welcome change of pace. I drove to the city of Sequim, meeting up with friends I'd made during my archaeology technician training program in California. Our easy, light-hearted conversation provided a much-needed respite from the solitude of recent hikes. As we walked together afterward, sharing stories and laughter, I was reminded that sometimes the best trails are the ones we share with others.

As I tallied the week's miles—45.8, barely scraping past my weekly goal—I realized something profound: the success part of my journey felt complete. Through these hundreds of miles, I'd thoroughly dismantled society's definition of success, rebuilding it around authenticity, vulnerability, and staying true to my values. But even as I checked off another week's mileage, a heavier question emerged: what about joy? That elusive quality I'd witnessed on Celeste's face seemed to have vanished completely in the gray mists of the Olympic Peninsula.

SOMETIMES JOY DISAPPEARS IN THE MIST.

As I trudged through the gray days of the Olympic Peninsula, I found myself grappling with a question that felt heavier than the grey skies overhead: What is the light that can pierce through the shadows? Hiking and immersing myself in nature had always been my steady sources of joy, yet suddenly, they weren't enough. That spark I so desperately needed seemed just out of reach.

The trails that once filled me with wonder now felt monotonous. Despite new adventures in Olympic National Park, my 1,000-mile quest had lost its luster. What was once a journey of discovery with my mentor, Celeste, now felt like a slog. Was I bored—or was this something deeper? Searching for clarity, I turned once again to Celeste, and her response arrived like a ray of sunlight through the clouds:

Dear Brenda,

Sometimes the path leads us through shadow valleys where joy seems to vanish completely. I know this place you're in—where even the most beautiful trail feels hollow, where every step is an effort, where the gray outside matches the gray within.

Don't try to force the light. Don't pretend to feel what isn't there. These shadow times have their own wisdom to teach us, if we're brave enough to sit with them.

Joy isn't a destination to reach or a goal to achieve. Perhaps it's not even something to seek. Perhaps joy is what emerges when we stop trying so hard, when we allow ourselves to simply be—even in the gray, even in the questioning, even in the not-knowing.

Let yourself be here, exactly as you are.

Keep walking your journey,

Celeste

Celeste's words hit home with unexpected force. This emotional landscape felt eerily familiar—I'd been here before, in those first months of RV life. Back then, I'd been stripped of all distractions, all routines, all ways of numbing myself to difficult emotions. Alone in my rig, I'd been forced to sit with my fears, my depression, my uncertainty. Each dawn brought a choice: hide from these feelings or face them head-on.

I remembered that February morning at Lake Corpus Christi State Park, in Texas, when I'd suddenly noticed the permanent smile on my face. Not because anything spectacular was happening—I was still scared, still uncertain about this nomadic life. But somehow, in allowing myself to feel everything fully, in stopping the endless running from discomfort, I'd stumbled upon something profound. I'd smiled more in those first months on the road than in the entire previous decade.

Now the Olympic Peninsula was pushing me back to that raw, uncomfortable space. The gray skies, the reserved trails, the monotonous miles—they were stripping away my defenses just as thoroughly as those early RV days had done. Each step felt heavy with questions: Why was I here? What was I really seeking? Where had my joy gone?

I began to wonder, is this deep sadness because of mom's health? Was I already prepping for her death, when so much life was ahead of me? Could I break through this shadow . . . at least enough to enjoy every conversation, every moment spent with mom. How could I get out of this funk, or was I simply destined to wait for sunny skies.

The "boring middle"—that's what I'd started calling this stretch of my quest. The initial excitement had faded, the finish line still felt distant, and I was left with the unglamorous work of simply showing up, day after day. No dramatic revelations, no mountain-top moments, just one foot in front of the other through the mist. But maybe this middle space had its own wisdom to offer. After all, life isn't lived in the peaks and valleys alone—it's lived in these in-between moments, these quiet stretches where transformation happens almost imperceptibly.

Maybe, these dark emotions signaled a turning point in my journey? I had released my stale dysfunctional definition of success. But joy? Maybe I'd been approaching it all wrong. Like success, I'd approached it as something to achieve, to check off my list of accomplishments. I'd imagined it as those peak moments—reaching a summit, conquering a fear, feeling that rush of accomplishment. But Celeste's kind of joy was different. Something in her seemed unshakeable, even in the midst of profound change.

The relentless gray of the Olympic Peninsula was teaching me something crucial: you can't chase joy any more than you can chase a shadow. Those early RV days had shown me this truth, though I'd forgotten it somewhere along the way. Joy hadn't come when I'd finally "figured out" RV life or conquered my fears. It had slipped in quietly, unexpectedly, after I'd stopped running from my emotions and simply allowed myself to be.

The path ahead still held mysteries. But for now, I would trust this shadow time, let it teach me what it would. After all, Celeste's radiance hadn't come from avoiding darkness—it had come from walking through it with complete honesty. Maybe that was the real journey I needed to take.

14.

LIGHTHOUSE LESSONS

Dates: August 18 – 24
Location: Olympic Peninsula, Washington
Trails: Fort Worden Historical State Park (Bluff Loop), HJ Carroll County Park, Larry Scott Trail, Dungeness Spit Trail
Miles Hiked in Week 14: 46.2
Total Miles Hiked: 692.9

WEEK 14 KICKED OFF with a rainstorm and a mini-disaster that felt all too symbolic of my current state. The wind, as if mirroring my internal turbulence, had torn my catio's tent shelter from its base. As I surveyed the damage, a wave of defeat washed over me. The repair job loomed large, and I just couldn't summon the energy to tackle it. Instead, I opted for a quick fix—bricks and sandbags to hold the floor in place. It wasn't perfect, and certainly not escape-proof—especially considering "Houdini's" talents—but it would have to do. Much like my emotional state, it was functional but fragile.

As if the catio mishap wasn't enough, my laptop malfunctioned. The battery started draining, even while plugged in, forcing me to shut it down and search for a computer repair shop. It was just one of those days, so I decided to stick close to home, walking my laps at the county park. Five miles later, I was back home, grateful for a peaceful end to a chaotic day.

If there's one thing I've learned about myself over these weeks on the trail, it's that I need at least one new adventure to mark each week. So, seizing a partly sunny Monday, I set out to walk the Dungeness Spit. My Midwestern roots prompted me to google "spit," only to discover that a spit is a stretch of beach that projects out to sea. And not just any spit—the Dungeness is the longest natural sand spit in North America, growing an impressive 13 feet per year.

My first stop was a computer repair shop in Sequim. As I stood outside the shop, located in a quaint downtown shopping center, my eyes were drawn to an enormous mural adorning the adjacent building. It was a vibrant depiction of local farm life, rich with charming details—cows and chickens peering out from barn doors, older women quilting on a porch, fields dotted with cattle, an old tractor, and the iconic pairing of a red barn and white farmhouse. But amidst this pastoral scene, something unusual caught my eye. Was that . . . a mastodon among the cattle? Later, I learned the mural commemorated a remarkable 1977 discovery when a local farmer unearthed mastodon bones in his field. The artist's clever integration of this prehistoric giant into the familiar farm scene was a stroke of whimsy.

This unexpected encounter with a painted mastodon catapulted me back to my days as a Virginia Master Naturalist. I remembered the exhilarating experience of helping prepare a real mastodon tusk for excavation and museum display. This little surprise lifted my mood, and I found myself smiling as I drove to the Dungeness Spit parking area.

The hike began with a half-mile paved trail through lush forest. As I emerged onto the beach, the vastness of sand and sea stretched before me, with no sign of the lighthouse that I knew lay five miles ahead. A chance encounter with a fellow solo woman RVer provided a welcome chat about the ups and downs of remote work—a brief connection in the solitude of the trail.

Arriving at low tide, I found the hard-packed sand perfect for the long trek to the New Dungeness Lighthouse. For miles, the lighthouse played tricks on me, seeming never to get closer despite my steady progress. But finally, I reached its white picket fence, greeted by a volunteer who ushered me inside. The narrow spiral staircase led me to the lantern room, rewarding my efforts with a breathtaking panoramic view of the Spit, Wildlife Refuge, Strait of Juan de Fuca, and Canada stretching out before me.

The lighthouse keepers, I learned, were volunteers who had paid for the privilege of spending a week in this isolated post. Their enthusiasm was contagious as they shared stories of watching last night's thunderstorms roll in and witnessing spectacular sunrises and sunsets. The commitment was no small feat—they're transported to the lighthouse on Saturdays, packed with everything they need for the week; a trip to town requires an eleven-mile round trip hike to the car.

As I began the long walk back, the rising tide forced me away from the shoreline, turning my pleasant stroll on hard sand into a more strenuous trek over dry, shifting sands and rocks. Despite the challenge, I felt a surge of gratitude for the sunshine and the unique experience. This lighthouse adventure had been a beacon in my week, reminding me that even in the midst of gloom, there are always new discoveries waiting to be made. And at 11.2 miles, this was one of my longest hikes and gave me a cushion for the rest of the week.

On occasion, I overstay my visit, and that's how I was beginning to see this last week in the Olympic Peninsula. I was more than ready to move on. The rest of the week's walks were routine—Port Townsend strolls, the Larry Scott Trail, and loops around the county park. On Saturday, amid periodic raindrops, I returned to my favorite trails at Fort Worden. But I had to admit, that old enemy, boredom, was sneaking up on me.

This week's weather tested my resolve, and I had to confront my "weather wimp" tendencies and the gloomy mood that I had sunk into. Despite the challenges, I'd managed to weave my walks between raindrops, clocking 46.2 miles for the week—just edging past my goal. My total mileage stood at 692.9 miles, tantalizingly close to the 700-mile milestone.

As I reflected on the week, I began to see the glimpses of joy perk through the dark skies. The soft purrs of my cats as they cuddled with me on a rainy day. The mastodon peering from a field of cows. The spiral staircase leading up to the lighthouse light. The vivid blue hydrangeas, dotted with rain drops. Maybe joy resides in the simple things, the everyday parts of life, if only we open our senses to it. Nature, I realized, held both life's mysteries and its lessons in resilience.

JOY THRIVES IN SIMPLICITY.

As I left the lighthouse behind, I couldn't shake how much those original keepers' lives spoke to me. They had chosen solitude, with a singular purpose—keeping the light burning, maintaining the beacon. No distractions, no competing priorities, just one clear mission. They watched storms roll in, witnessed spectacular sunrises, and kept watch over the bay.

Simplicity. Maybe that's where I had gone wrong—always trying to do more than expected, to juggle multiple projects, and to feel some level of twisted pride in how much I could get done. My thoughts drifted back to last summer's travels and an impromptu stop at the Northern Great Lakes Visitor Center in Wisconsin. There I learned about the Anishinaabe Seven Fires prophecy, which speaks of humanity standing at a critical crossroads.

The prophecy describes two distinct paths. The Hard Path represents unbridled technological progress and materialism, leading to pollution, destruction, and imbalance. It's a path of constant acceleration—social, political, economic, environmental, and spiritual. The Soft Path offers a slower journey of enlightenment and spiritual reconnection with nature, recognizing the spirit in all things—water, air, Earth, plants, animals, and humans alike. According to the prophecy, today's natural disasters—volcanos, wildfires, floods, hurricanes—serve as urgent messages calling us to choose wisely between these paths.

Mom's decision to forgo further treatment seemed to embody the Soft Path philosophy. Back home, her surgical wound was healing nicely, and my brother had stepped into the role of caregiver, allowing my sister to return to Tennessee. Together with my younger brother, they'd moved mom's bedroom downstairs, easing her daily routine. She was thriving in these simpler circumstances—even passing my brother's impromptu driving test. She spent more time with the grandkids and planned to return to swimming soon. Her choice represented a natural approach to her remaining days, choosing quality of life over the Hard Path of endless appointments, invasive tests, machines, and medications.

The prophecy resonated deeply with me, not just as a warning for humanity, but as a mirror of my own crossroads. Would I return to the fast-paced world of business, or choose a slower, more mindful path? The urgency of the prophecy added weight to my decision, reminding me that my personal choices could have far-reaching consequences. I knew deep in my heart that the Soft Path, in all its purity, was a thing of the past. Technology invades every aspect of my life, from fueling up the RV to emailing my sisters to tracking my hikes.

Maybe the true question was how to honor and nurture the Soft Path within our modern world?

And maybe it's simplicity that forms the core of that response? Simplicity requires prioritizing, much like the process I used to transfer my most important belongings to my motorhome. What held sentimental value and was transportable? What would I need in my daily living? Downsizing. Prioritizing. Simplifying. Could these same processes be used to navigate joy? These were the questions I asked Celeste, and with her usual brevity, she responded in her latest postcard.

Dear Brenda,

Your lighthouse keepers understood something vital—that focus creates power. Their single beam, cutting through fog and darkness, guides ships safely home not by illuminating everything, but by shining steadily on what matters most.

In our scattered world, we're told to diversify, multitask, spread ourselves across platforms and purposes. But there's profound strength in simplicity, in doing one thing with your whole heart.

What would your life look like if you directed your energy like that lighthouse beam— not trying to light the entire ocean, but focusing your unique brilliance where it can truly make a difference?

Shine your light where it matters most,

Celeste

Celeste's words illuminated something I'd been missing. Like those lighthouse keepers with their singular focus, joy doesn't come from doing everything possible—it emerges from doing what matters most. As I thought about joy, memories flashed through my mind. What brought joy to my life? Hiking and being immersed in nature were the obvious answers. And then there were those perfect moments when everything aligned, etching themselves forever in my memory.

My most vivid experience of joy occurred more than 20 years ago. After adopting my child from Ukraine, my parents visited for the first time. During a weekend at the beach, we unexpectedly found ourselves caught in a parade crowd. I lifted my child onto my shoulders, and in that ordinary moment, I found myself choking back tears. Finally, I was a mom. We were family. Pure, unexpected joy washing over me in the midst of a simple day.

And maybe joy really is that simple. Walking down the street holding a loved one's hand. Watching a butterfly emerge from its cocoon. Standing barefoot on the beach. Smelling the sweet aroma of the desert after a soft rain. But it begs the question—if it's those simple things that bring pleasure, why do we spend most of our time in a chaotic world filled with busyness and competing interests?

The wisdom in Celeste's words felt like a key turning in a lock. I'd been approaching my future as if it were a multiple-choice test where I had to circle all the right answers. But what if it was more like the lighthouse—one clear beam cutting through the fog? The thought of returning to my business, of juggling multiple roles and responsibilities, suddenly felt like an unnecessary complication.

The relentless gray of the Olympic Peninsula was teaching me something crucial about clarity. When you can't see the whole horizon, you focus on the next step ahead. I thought about the keeper's commitment to their weekly post, about the prophecy's call to choose between paths, about the mastodon's warning against unsustainable complexity.

As I walked through another misty morning, my path began to clarify. What if my future was just one thing? Nurturing the Earth and thriving within its majesty. Maybe, like the lighthouse keepers, I didn't need to illuminate the entire ocean—I just needed to focus my beam on one specific part: guiding other to live more simply on this Earth. The shape of this commitment was still forming, but I could feel it calling to me through the mist—writing, volunteering, sharing what I'd learned about finding joy in a simpler life.

The future remains a hazy horizon, but one thing has become clear—the simple life I've cultivated on the road isn't a temporary escape; it's my path forward. I'm learning that joy doesn't come from doing everything possible, but from doing what matters most. The skies may not have cleared yet, but I've stopped trying to see down every trail. Sometimes one clear beam of light is all we need to find our way home.

15.

UNEXPECTED CONNECTIONS

Dates: August 25 – 31
Location: Western Washington
Trails: Fort Worden Historical State Park (Bluff Loop), HJ Carroll County Park, Centennial Trail, Explorer Falls, Snoqualmie River Trail
Miles Hiked in Week 15: 46.1
Total Miles Hiked: 739.0

THE MORNING FOG hung low as I prepared to leave the Olympic Peninsula, squeezing in a final walk on the Bluff Trail at Fort Worden with a fellow RVer from my California resort. I checked my phone reflexively—no missed calls from home—before pocketing it and turning back to the trail. As we paused to catch our breath at the overlook, I reflected on the month's experiences—the surprising dog bite, the awe-inspiring whale encounter in Canada, the challenging hike to Lake Angeles, my trek to the Dungeness Lighthouse, countless strolls around Port Townsend. On paper, it had been a great month. Yet something felt amiss, a persistent hollowness that even reaching the 700-mile mark couldn't fill.

My friend, noticing my distant gaze, spoke softly. "Maybe you're depressed." The words hung in the air between us. "Yes," I admitted, "I guess I am." But why? My hiking quest was progressing well—I'd just reached the 700-mile mark. I was witnessing breathtaking sights, writing, exploring. Yet my energy had bottomed out. I couldn't deny that I was saddened by the "long goodbye" I would soon have to bid mom. While I'd wrestled with depression before, particularly in my early thirties, this felt different. The grey Washington skies seemed to have seeped into my bones, weighing me down even as my feet continued to carry me forward on the trail.

That evening, as I prepared the rig for departure, I couldn't shake our conversation. The simple things may bring joy, but as much as I tried to focus on my soft footsteps on the wet grass or the flight of a hummingbird as it sucked the nectar from a petunia, a touch of emptiness, and loneliness, stayed with me. At the same time, I was hopeful. Perhaps a new location with unexplored trails will rejuvenate my mood? Plus, I had just reached 700 miles! I was truly on the back side of this journey.

Monday dawned with the promise of a new chapter. After squeezing in a couple of farewell loops around the county park, I hit the road. After an easy drive, I tucked my rig into a snug site among towering trees at my new home, Flowing Lake County Park in the Puget Sound region. A short stroll to the lake delivered a view that was pure magic—giant conifers perfectly mirrored in still waters. As the sun disappeared on the horizon, I studied the local hiking trails, wondering if my smiles and energy would naturally return? A quick check of the weather showed sunny days ahead. Perhaps this was the jumpstart my mood needed.

The biggest town near Flowing Lake County Park was Snohomish, a town of about 10,000 souls. The area offered diverse trails within an hour's drive, and I spent my first two days exploring the Centennial Trail, a converted railbed that provided easy walking and glimpses of downtown. But these walks introduced me to another quirk of Washington culture—silent, speeding cyclists who seemed allergic to announcing their presence. Out of thirty riders, only two called out or rang a bell. My walks on paved trails only made me crave the soft Earth beneath my feet.

As I recorded my mileage, I noticed a definite slowdown in my pace. While I was confident I would reach my goal for the week, I was no longer piling up the big numbers. And I couldn't remember the last time I had simply wandered, walking for fun rather than exercise. So on Thursday, I took myself out to the Evergreen State Fair.

As I entered the fairgrounds, I was reminded of the timeless quality of county fairs, a familiarity that transcends age. The vibrant red, white, and yellow booths offering cotton candy and popcorn; the expansive barns and show rings for animals; the whirling Tilt-a-Whirl in all its variations; the enticing games of chance; and excited children with sticky hands. These sights and sounds transported me back to my childhood, when August meant the county fair and Labor Day weekend brought the rides and beer tents of Marathon Fun Days. In my mind, fairs were synonymous with cheese curds, live music, and carefree fun with friends.

Yet here I was, alone at the fair, just as I am alone in life. I'd be lying if I said I didn't yearn for companionship, especially in this environment teeming with families and groups of friends. But I was determined to enjoy myself nonetheless. I wandered through the barns, pausing to listen to a band cover Cyndi Lauper's "Girls Just Wanna Have Fun." The wide variety of chickens on display captivated me, their diverse colors and sizes a testament to nature's creativity. In the llama and alpaca barn, I found myself in an unexpected stare-down with a llama, its intense gaze both intimidating and amusing. My animal tour continued, falling in love with a Rex rabbit, greeting a newborn calf, and marveling at the magnificent Clydesdale horses.

As the day wore on, I found myself at the farmer's market, alive with vendors and solo shoppers. Here, I felt more at ease, scoring some sourdough bread and fresh farm eggs. That evening's walk around the campground reminded me why I'd come to Washington in the first place—to explore its trails.

On Friday, I experienced a bit of magic, compliments of Mother Nature. And maybe it was just the thing to pull me out of my funk? I was back on soft earth, hiking the forest service road to Explorer Falls. I had the place to myself, and I relished the sound of birds singing and the warm sun shining overhead. A careful creek crossing led me to the falls and a hidden cave dubbed the "Hobbit Hole." After weeks of grey, this taste of wilderness felt like a balm for my soul.

On my return trek, I stood atop a tree stump, peering at the distant mountains. And that's when I saw it. The breeze had picked up and ahead of me, for as far as I could see, were fields of fireweed, scattering their seeds like summer snowflakes. I waved at an approaching family, asking the kids if they brought their mittens! We shared a laugh, and once I was alone again, I did a little twirl, seeds falling all around me. The joy was back, if only for a moment.

On Saturday, I drove the backroads of Washington to the charming town of Duvall. I was surprised to see a sign saying I was in King County, the same county as Seattle, even though I felt a thousand miles away from the city. I found a parking spot and walked on the Snoqualmie Valley Trail, a 32-mile gravel path on an old railroad grade that weaved through farmland and buzzed with weekend bikers. After three miles, I turned back, feeling satisfied with a week well spent.

As Week 15 drew to a close, the numbers told a story of steady progress. Despite a travel day, I had met my goal, reaching 46.1 miles for the week. This pushed my grand total to 739 miles—a figure that filled me with both pride and anticipation. The "boring middle" of my quest seemed to be behind me, and I could almost glimpse the finish line on the horizon.

As the sunshine brought back a glimpse of joy, I thought about the importance of connections. Not just connections to people, but connecting to nature, and to our very souls. And maybe, that was the missing ingredient as I move forward on my journey.

JOY GROWS THROUGH CONNECTION.

While wandering through the crowds at the fair had left me feeling disconnected, another moment during the week showed me how quickly that feeling could change. All it took was the courage to reach out.

Have you ever noticed how the simplest gesture can bridge the widest gap? That's what happened to me on the Centennial Trail. As I walked, hugging the right shoulder, I noticed two older women approaching, seemingly oblivious to trail etiquette as they headed straight for me. Initially, I felt a twinge of irritation. But then, a thought struck me: Maybe there's a reason for their behavior. And in that moment, I decided to let my playful side take the lead.

As we approached the collision stage, I called out, "well, since you're walking on my side of the trail, you must want a hug." I opened my arms wide, and to my delight, they broke into smiles. One of the women mirrored my gesture, and we embraced, sharing a hearty laugh, the unexpected moment of connection brightening the day for all of us.

As we parted, I detected an accent in the woman's voice. She hesitantly revealed she was Israeli, quickly following up with a cautious, "Is that okay?"

The tension in her voice was palpable. Without hesitation, I assured her that in my worldview, we are all humans sharing the same planet. The relief that washed over her face was immediate and profound. That small moment of connection had cut through every cultural and personal barrier—like sunshine through fog.

This spontaneous act of openness had taken me by surprise. It felt liberating, a reminder that I didn't have to remain trapped in feelings of disconnection and sadness. I had the power within me to change the energy around me, to brighten someone else's day with a simple smile and an unexpected hug. As I walked my evening loop around the campground, each step brought fresh clarity. What if connection wasn't just about chance encounters or shared moments? What if it was about maintaining our bonds even as they transform, about finding new ways to touch hearts across time and space?

As the sun set over Flowing Lake, I reflected on Mom's approach to her illness. While I struggled with the weight of anticipatory grief, she continued embracing each day, finding small moments of joy despite her prognosis. She spoke animatedly about games with the grandkids and cherished visits from friends. Mom's unwavering spirit offered a profound lesson: joy isn't dependent on circumstances but on how we choose to meet them. In her quiet courage, she was teaching me one final, essential truth about living fully, even as time grew short.

As the sky deepened into oranges and pinks, a postcard from Celeste seemed to materialize in my pocket.

Dear Brenda,

Joy isn't just about lighthearted moments—it's about connection, the invisible threads we weave between ourselves and the world. And yes, those threads are fragile, sometimes slipping through our fingers before we're ready. But that doesn't mean joy disappears.

What matters isn't how much joy we feel, but how we let it flow through us and into the world. Every interaction, no matter how brief, creates ripples of possibility. Your mother's joy flows through you, just as yours flows into others. That's the real magic of connection—it transforms us even as we transform others.

Trust in these invisible threads of joy that bind us all together. They're stronger than distance, more enduring than grief.

Keep reaching. Keep connecting. Joy will always find its way back to you.

Celeste

I spent a long time that evening watching the light fade over the lake, my feet pressed firmly against the earth. A pair of ducks glided in for a landing, their wings catching the last golden rays. In that moment, I felt the truth of what Celeste had written about energy and connection. We're all just vessels really, temporary carriers of something larger than ourselves. My mother's energy would indeed someday float back into the universe, but perhaps that's not an ending—just a different form of connection.

The thought brought unexpected peace. We each carry our own energy into the world—some bring joy, others sadness, many a complex mixture of both. The Israeli woman had brought vulnerability and warmth, turning a moment of tension into connection. Even the silent cyclists contributed their own energy to my journey, making me question my assumptions about human nature. I thought about how my own energy affected others—how a simple gesture like opening my arms for a hug could transform not just my day, but someone else's too.

This wasn't just about being positive or negative, happy or sad. It was about understanding that what we put out into the world creates ripples, like stones dropped in Flowing Lake. Some days I carried grief's heavy weight, other days hope's buoyant lift. Both were valid, both part of being human. What mattered was staying conscious of the energy I brought to each encounter, each moment.

My own offering, perhaps, was simply staying open to it all. Open to the joy of spontaneous hugs, to the ache of impending loss, to the mystery of connections that transcend distance and time. Standing there by the lake, watching the last light fade from the sky, I finally understood something else about joy. It isn't just about the connections we make—it's about recognizing that we're already connected, all of us, in ways that no distance or darkness can ever really break.

16.

THE RHYTHM OF DISCOVERY

Dates: September 1 – 7
Location: Western Washington
Trails: Lord Hill Regional Park, Bayview Trail, Bridle Trails State Park, Wallace Falls State Park, Lime Kiln Trail, Robe Canyon Historic Trail, Tolt Pipeline Trail
Miles Hiked in Week 16: 54.4
Total Miles Hiked: 794.4

LAST WEEK'S DANCE under the falling seedlings set a tone for the new week. Could I turn that flicker of joy and lightheartedness into a glowing flame? This would be my last full week in Washington, and after looking at the numbers, I realized that I might just be able to reach the 800-mile mark before leaving the state. Setting that goal felt like a prod to take the trails more seriously, and push myself physically. Somehow, things had gotten easy, and this new challenge reenergized me.

The week began with an excursion to Lord Hill Regional Park, a tapestry of trails offering both a view of the Snohomish River and sweeping mountain vistas. My journey started with an uphill climb on an old gravel road, followed by a steep ascent promising panoramic views. At the overlook, an unexpected sight caught my eye—a colorfully painted rock bearing the message, "Find Stillness." This simple yet profound instruction seemed to challenge my growing fixation on reaching my mileage goals. Already, I felt the tension between moving forward and pausing to absorb the moment—a theme that would weave through my entire week.

As I navigated the trails, the constant hum of distant freeway traffic served as a reminder of the world beyond the park. However, descending towards the more secluded river paths, the urban soundtrack faded, replaced by the forest's natural orchestra. At the river's edge, I paused, allowing the soothing sounds of flowing water to wash over me. A small airplane perched near the riverbank piqued my curiosity—how did it manage to land in such a confined space? Despite this touch of human presence, the hike offered a welcome change of scenery and a breath of fresh air.

The next two days brought rain and overcast skies, forcing me to adapt. On Monday, after running errands, I discovered a sign for Bayview Trail. It was nothing more than an urban walking path winding its way through the suburbs. Its paved, hilly route offered occasional glimpses of the bay, and a friendly encounter with a wandering cat added warmth to the grey day.

But the turn-around point offered a stark reminder of hardships. At the bus stop sat an older gentleman, dressed in layers of shabby clothing, shopping cart loaded with all his belongings. We exchanged looks, and just like that, memories flooded back. The constant worries of how to pay the rent, how long my jar of peanut butter would last, and fears about needing healthcare. I could see that the light in his eyes had dimmed, just as mine had at one time. We may not need much, but safe shelter and food are top on the hierarchy of needs. Gratitude flooded me, and I wished him well as I returned to my Jeep.

Tuesday's persistent rain confined me to the campground, where I took three separate walks around the grounds, to the lake, and down the road to meet my mileage goal. And with this more causal pace, I felt myself tugged toward that that message of "Find Stillness." I made a compromise to myself. Reach those 800 miles. . . and then, slow down. Focus more on the journey, less on the miles.

With sunny skies returning midweek, I ventured to Bridle Trails State Park in Kirkland. True to its name, the park featured a corral and welcomed equestrians. Wide trails and cute signage—a paw print for Cougar trail, a flower for Trillium trail—added to its charm. Despite its urban location, the mid-week solitude made me feel as if I'd stumbled into a vast, secluded forest. And for a bonus, I found a Trader Joe's nearby, giving me the chance to stock up on my favorites.

Thursday's adventure took me to Wallace Falls State Park on a glorious sunny day. The trail began beneath enormous, buzzing power lines, their ominous presence spurring thoughts of cancer risks and hastening my pace towards the forest. Wallace Falls showcased a trio of cascades—lower, middle, and upper falls—each with its own character and voice. The lower falls rumbled with steady determination. The upper falls, though imposing in height, remained partially hidden behind a veil of trees. But it was the middle falls that captured my imagination.

Standing on the bridge over Wallace River, I felt the mist on my face as I paused to take photos. The middle falls spread wide across the rock face, water dancing over countless unseen channels before gathering its courage to leap. Here, the river seemed to pause in its downward journey, gathering itself in pools before continuing its descent—neither rushing headlong like the upper falls nor settled into routine like the lower section. It was a lovely day, and the sunshine brought out friendlier hikers and more smiles than I had encountered on other Washington trails.

I was meeting my daily mileage goal, but with three days left, I had to kick up the mileage if I wanted to reach that 800-mile mark in Washington. Friday's plans for Lime Kiln trail went awry when my GPS led me astray and cell service vanished. Undeterred, I pivoted to the Robe Canyon Historic Trail I'd passed earlier. Without a downloaded map, I committed to sticking to the main trail and turning back if conditions became dicey. The path began with a forest descent to the river's edge, where I paused to record the serene view from the riverbed rocks. About a mile and a half in, the trail turned rocky and steep. After navigating a fallen tree, I encountered a sign warning of a trail closure due to landslides and unsafe conditions. One glance at the steep canyon walls and the trail's isolation was enough to send me back.

On the return drive, a sign for Granite Falls caught my eye. The short trail to the falls revealed a local hangout marred by graffiti-covered rocks and structures. As I read about the salmon ladders, I couldn't help but ponder the disconnect between humans and nature that leads to such vandalism.

In a twist of fate, as I was leaving Granite Falls, I spotted a sign for the elusive Lime Kiln Trail. With daylight and energy to spare, I couldn't resist. The hike led me to a historic stone kiln once used for lime production, transported by a narrow-gauge railway. As I trekked alongside the river, I marveled at how this rugged path could have ever accommodated a train. The trail's muddiness beyond the kiln marked my turnaround point, capping off a three-trail hiking day.

Saturday brought another curveball when construction crews blocked the parking area near my intended trailhead. Adapting once again, I found myself on the Tolt Pipeline Trail East. This mowed path adjacent to the pipeline offered expansive views of rolling hills, punctuated by nearby horse farms and the occasional rooster crow. A friendly dog walker warned me of a recent bear sighting, prompting a quick check of my bear spray. Sure enough, I spotted bear scat on my return walk. Despite the potential wildlife encounter, the peaceful 11-mile trek was a fitting end to a week of unexpected discoveries.

These sunny day adventures boosted my spirits and revealed a pattern in my exploration. With each detour and unexpected discovery—from hidden historic kilns to painted rocks on the trail—I felt a childlike thrill that had been missing in those dreary, rain-soaked days. It wasn't just the sunshine that brightened my mood; it was the constant invitation to wonder what might be around the next corner. Like picking up a colorful stone or climbing a hill to see the other side, my journey had become a treasure hunt guided by an insatiable question: what will I find next?

CURIOSITY IS THE INSTIGATOR OF JOY.

On Friday, I reconnected with Mitch, the "Man on the Dock" at Wizard Island in Crater Lake, on his podcast. As a guest, we talked about adventures on the road and the meaning of success. I could hear my voice grow in excitement as I talked about the trails, sights, adventures, and people I met on my travels. This was one of the ways I fed my curiosity, and by stepping out of my routine, the dimensions of my life took form. Even my connection to Mitch was an outcome of curiosity—and my boldness to call out to a stranger.

As our discussion continued, I was drawn to the factor that often separates people: Action. What good is curiosity if it doesn't spark action? And just like that, I had a conundrum on my hands. On the one hand, that message on the rock to "Find Stillness" resonated with me. On the other hand, action calls out to me. I have to satisfy that curiosity. Are stillness and action oppositional? Or could they possibly be complementary? And if so, how does that fit into curiosity and joy?

Maybe the answer was in front of me? I thought about my hike in Wallace Falls State Park. Like most trails, I alternated between moments of movement and moments of pause. I'd push forward, propelled by curiosity about what lay around the next bend, then stop completely, absorbed in the details of a moss-covered log or the pattern of water cascading over rocks.

When curiosity calls you forward to discover what lies beyond the next hill, you move. When wonder invites you to absorb the details of a moment—the pattern of bark on a tree, the conversation of birds, the message on a painted rock—you pause. Both states—action and stillness—seemed essential to my experience.

At the middle falls viewpoint, I paused longer than usual. The thundering water created a natural amphitheater of sound, drawing me into a state of heightened awareness. In that moment of physical stillness, my mind wasn't idle but acutely receptive—noticing how the water's path changed as it navigated around rocks, observing the gradual meandering of the downhill stream, feeling the subtle vibrations through the viewing platform beneath my feet.

This wasn't the passive stillness of boredom or disengagement. It was an active receptivity, a state of being fully present that allowed me to absorb details I might have missed if I'd kept moving. And it struck me that perhaps stillness and action weren't opposing forces but complementary phases in the cycle of curiosity and discovery.

As I pondered these questions, I observed Mom's approach to life. Despite our gentle prompting toward hospice care, she maintained her routines—playing piano at the assisted living center, visiting friends, and embracing each day. Who were we to tell her how she should feel or act?

Each week at the center, she played piano by heart for an appreciative audience, bringing out old songs from her childhood and fulfilling requests. What song would pop into her mind next? Could she remember how to play it? These simple pleasures kept her engaged with life, regardless of her prognosis.

Without intending to, Mom demonstrated this balance between action and stillness. Her activities expressed engagement with life, while the moments of stillness came between the notes—in the pauses where she listened to requests

121

or searched her memory for melodies. She wasn't denying death; she was embracing life with both movement and pause, in her own rhythm.

Curiosity prompts action—we move toward what intrigues us, whether physically, intellectually, or emotionally. But without moments of stillness to absorb and process what we find, our discoveries remain surface-level. Stillness, in turn, allows space for new curiosities to emerge, sparking the next movement.

My mind flashed back to my first glimpse of Celeste, quietly absorbing the beauty of the turquoise waters from her seat on the ferry. Curiosity, with a blend of fierce determination, brought her to the island. She saw life as a gift, something to be treasured and explored. And maybe that was the outgrowth of a deep curiosity that fueled her inner being. On Saturday night, as I calculated the miles needed to reach 800 before leaving Washington, I imagined what Celeste might say in a postcard from her wanderings.

Dear Brenda,

Remember seeing the world as a five-year-old? Every leaf held possibility, every stone might hide treasure. That's the secret to lasting joy—preserving wonder as we age.

Curiosity is our natural state, but we often trade it for comfort. Joy lives in the questions, not the answers. It thrives when we take unfamiliar trails, talk to strangers, or pause to examine what we'd normally pass by.

Your mother understands this—it's why she finds delight despite everything. It's also what drew you to me on that ferry. You recognized someone who hadn't let age dim her wonder.

The waterfall you admired embodies this perfectly—powerful in its flow yet peaceful in its presence. You're learning this dance too—how to balance motion and stillness, seeking and finding, effort and surrender.

Keep turning stones and seeing the world with fresh eyes. That's where joy finds you.

Stay curious,

Celeste

As I lay in bed, listening to raindrops on the roof, I thought about the rhythm of discovery that had shaped my life. My memories took me back to a corn field on the family farm after harvest. I remember walking through the empty field, discovering colorful "Indian corn" left behind, delighting in the shape, texture, and rainbow of kernels. That same wonder had followed me into adulthood, and I'd seen it reflected in my child's eyes as we explored neighborhood Halloween decorations years later.

This childhood wonder wasn't something I'd lost and rediscovered on the trail—it had been there all along, sometimes buried under responsibilities, sometimes dimmed by hardship, but never extinguished. The courage to follow curiosity required both the boldness to act and the patience to be still and receptive.

This rhythm extended beyond hiking. My conversations with Mom balanced animation and quiet. My writing alternated between periods of creative flow and reflective editing. Even my decision to embark on this RV journey had required both the action of making a bold change and the stillness to listen to what my heart truly wanted.

Perhaps this was the secret to sustainable joy—not choosing between stillness and action, but honoring both as essential parts of a curious life. The painted rock hadn't been telling me to stop moving but to incorporate moments of conscious stillness into my journey. And my drive to explore wasn't at odds with reflection but enhanced by it.

As I prepared for my final day in Washington, I felt a renewed sense of purpose. I would reach my goal, and then it would be time to explore new horizons. The excitement of travel was back.

17.

THE TIDES OF TIME

Dates: September 8 – 14
Location: Western Washington, Oregon Coast
Trails: Pilchuk River Trail, Rockaway Beach
Miles Hiked in Week 17: 40.1
Total Miles Hiked: 834.5

SUNDAY SHOWED THE promise of sunny skies, and I was buoyed by the fact that I was just 5.6 miles away from reaching the 800-mile mark. It was my final day in Washington, and a leisurely walk along the river sounded like the perfect way to end this leg of my journey. My destination: the Pilchuk River Trail. Little did I know that this last Washington trek would provide a stark contrast to the rhythm I was about to discover on the Oregon coast.

I could not have predicted the abrupt start to my easy woodland walk along an old logging road. As I set out, two women and their dog were heading back, warning of gunshots they'd heard further along. It wasn't hunting season and they didn't know of any nearby gun ranges, adding an edge of unease to the air. I headed out, knowing I can always turn around, and found solace in the river's gentle flow and the satisfying crunch of autumn leaves beneath my feet. No gunshots.

The trail, however, fell short of expectations. Only a brief moment allowed me to step onto the riverbed, a fleeting connection with the water I'd hoped to follow. But it was the trail's end that truly struck me—a clearcut hill, stripped bare of vegetation. The stark contrast with the lush, forested hills nearby was jarring, almost nauseating. This abrupt transition from nature's abundance to man's devastation felt like a punch to the gut.

As I turned back, my mind kept circling back to the devastation I'd witnessed. Must progress always come at nature's expense? Have we become so disconnected from the magic of the natural world that we carelessly wipe out entire forests, deface waterfalls with graffiti, and litter trails with plastic bottles? While most of my hikes had been on well-maintained state or federal lands, these more accessible trails near urban areas often bore the scars of human disrespect. It felt like a grim affirmation that we were indeed on the "hard path" of the Seventh Fire prophecy, hurtling towards environmental destruction if we fail to change course.

This final Washington hike should have been cause for celebration—I'd reached the significant milestone of 800 miles. Instead, it felt symbolic in a different, more somber way. Perhaps it encapsulated some of the gloomier days I'd experienced mid-quest. I'd approached the trail with hope and anticipation, only to encounter warnings and an ominous scene at its end. The experience left me ready to shake off the gloom.

As I packed up my rig for the long drive to the Oregon coast, I looked at my numbers. I hiked 801.5 miles in 113 days—an average of 7.1 miles per day— almost 50 miles per week. I was ahead of schedule. A new challenge lay ahead: Could I slow down, take my foot off the accelerator, and appreciate the journey all that much more?

Monday morning brought a sense of relief as I hitched up my Jeep and began the long slog through Seattle and Tacoma traffic. Despite the congestion, I felt lighter with each mile. I was leaving the dark forest behind, both literally and metaphorically, with the promise of ten days alongside the mighty Pacific Ocean ahead. The contrast couldn't have been more stark—from the enclosed, sometimes oppressive forest to the open expanse of the ocean. It felt like a symbolic transition, not just in my journey, but in my state of mind.

As I crossed into Oregon, steering my rig westward, the landscape unfolded before me like a painter's masterpiece. Sandy beaches intermingled with rocky shorelines, while massive rocks stood sentinel in the water. The bays bustled with fishing boats, their activity punctuating the pockets of water created by nature's sculptural land formations. My anticipation grew as I drove to the county campground near Rockaway Beach, my heart leaping at the realization that I could walk to the beach directly from my campsite.

I set up camp and headed to the beach, where I slipped off my sandals and dug my feet in the sand. Last week's lesson of motion and stillness were captured in that moment. The ocean was in constant motion, but there I stood, listening to the roar of the waves, watching the birds fly overhead, and soaking in the sunshine. Stillness among motion. And my curiosity was piqued. What would this stretch of coastline reveal to someone ready to move at a different pace?

The beach became my new trail, infinitely more forgiving than the forest paths I'd left behind. The sand between my toes—the tactile connection with the earth—rejuvenated me. My daily walks took me from the jetty to Twin Rocks, two colossal stone sentinels rising from the sea. It wasn't until my second trek that I discovered the hidden magic: viewed from beyond, one of the rocks revealed an arch, framing the crashing waves like nature's own picture window.

Twin Rocks seemed to part the ocean, creating a mesmerizing wave pattern on the shore. This interplay of elements—the irresistible force of water meeting the immovable rocks—served as a powerful reminder of nature's dynamics. These opposing forces coexisted, yes, but in doing so, they transformed the entire beach beyond.

My coastal sojourn brought an unexpected delight in the form of the Tillamook Creamery. Through expansive glass windows, I watched the cheese-making process from a bird's eye view. But the true highlight? The ice cream, of course. I found myself drawn back to the creamery twice during my stay, each visit culminating in a cone of their creamery-exclusive marionberry swirl. These small indulgences, I realized, added a dash of sweetness to what could have been ordinary days.

As the week progressed, the weather became a partner in my lessons about rhythm and change. The brilliant blue skies and sunshine gradually yielded to coastal gray. On Thursday, I was determined to capture a vivid Pacific sunset, but instead, I was greeted with a blanket of mist, and the sunset was more of a dim sigh than a glowing spectacle. By Saturday, my rain jacket became my companion as I returned to the beach to watch a lone fisherman test his luck in the drizzle. Even the elements seemed to be teaching me about the futility of demanding constant perfection, showing instead the beauty in nature's own unhurried cycles.

If it's possible to experience a beach "high" without any assistance, that's precisely where I found myself. The atmosphere was a stark contrast to the somber Washington forest hikes; each person I encountered on the beach offered a friendly "hi" or a wave. I walked with a lightness in my step, my smile as bright as the sun overhead.

On Friday, as I reached my Twin Rocks turn-around point, I paused to gaze out at the ocean. There, riding the waves, was a fishing boat. In a moment of whimsy, my mind conjured up an image of Celeste on that boat. There she was, waving madly with a huge grin on her face, her voice somehow carrying over the crash of waves: "You're doing great, Brenda!" I found myself waving back, thinking, "It's great to see you again, Celeste."

I closed the week with 40.1 miles, falling 5.4 miles short of my weekly goal. This included a mere 2.2 miles on my travel day, a conscious choice to embrace a slower pace. My total now stood at 834.5 miles, a figure that filled me with both pride and contemplation. As I watched the waves endlessly approach and retreat from the shore, a truth emerged clear as the horizon line.

JOY IS MAKING PEACE WITH THE PASSAGE OF TIME.

As I walked the shoreline each day, I became acutely aware of how the beach transformed with the tides. At low tide, the expanse of sand stretched out before me, seemingly limitless—firm, walkable, inviting exploration. Hours later, that same stretch would disappear beneath the surging water, forcing a different path, a different pace. This daily metamorphosis began to feel like a profound metaphor for the passage of time.

In youth, life feels like perpetual low tide—time stretching endlessly before us, days unfurling with limitless possibility. We can dig our toes in the sand, pause to examine every shell, believing the expanse will last forever. We rarely consider the tide's inevitable turn, the gradual compression of our temporal shoreline.

The middle years—with their whirlwind of work, parenthood, and responsibilities—feel like constant high tide. We leap from rock to rock, balance precariously on driftwood, racing through life to keep our heads above water. Time accelerates, days blur into months, then years. We find ourselves gasping, "Where did the time go?" as if it had been stolen rather than spent.

Now, no longer in life's middle, I feel a sense of calm, acceptance, and often, quiet urgency. It's as if I'm walking in the transition zone. Some days, I catch just the end of low tide, soaking in life's grandeur before stepping to higher ground. Other days, as high tide recedes, I transition from hurried rock-hopping to a casual beach stroll.

When I tallied my week's miles and found myself more than five miles short of my goal, I could feel the low rumbling of anxiety set in. I was committed to slowing down, and I was miles ahead of my schedule. I had time to spare, so why was I worried?

Then came a radical thought that stopped me in my tracks: What if I stopped the quest entirely?

The idea was simultaneously liberating and terrifying. I'd already proven I could do it. Did I really need to remain tethered to my mileage chart? What if I simply walked when I wanted to, free from the constraints of recording every step?

I sat with this thought, examining it from all angles. Would abandoning the quest feel like freedom or failure? Would I be honoring my deeper wisdom or simply giving up?

Almost immediately, the answer rose from deep within with a resounding "Hell, no!" I realized I genuinely enjoyed every aspect of this quest, including my weekly goals. The structure, the challenge, the sense of purpose—all had become integral to my journey. I could adjust the pace, perhaps, but abandoning the rhythm altogether held no appeal.

On one of my morning walks, a set of perfectly shaped footprints in the sand had caught my eye. I'd paused to photograph the image, sharing it online with the caption "a picture of happiness." But the photo revealed an unexpected optical illusion—what should have been an imprint appeared to stand atop the sand. This mind-bending visual struck me as profoundly metaphorical. Our time on earth is but a brief impression in the cosmic sand—here, then gone with the next tide. Yet the marks we leave—our actions, our relationships, the lives we touch—somehow persist beyond our physical presence, standing atop rather than merely imprinted in the world we briefly inhabit.

I called my mom during one of my beach walks. I laughed as she shared the news of her Bingo winnings. There she was, sticking to her routines, spending time with friends, and enjoying life. Mom had found her own way to face mortality—neither racing to complete a bucket list nor surrendering to inactivity. Instead, she moved at a pace that brought her joy, that felt authentic to who she had always been.

Looking down the beach, I watched people move along the shore. Some marched with purpose, headphones on, eyes forward. Others meandered slowly, stopping frequently to examine treasures at their feet. I watched a pony-tailed little girl carry wet sand in her bucket, determined to create her own masterpiece on the shore. Each person walked according to their own inner timekeeper—some racing against the imagined clock, others surrendering completely to the eternal now.

While I can't control the tides of time, this awareness grants me the freedom to make intentional decisions about how to navigate them. What if the secret of life is simply choosing when and how to walk the beach? Tide charts provide all the necessary information. Most days, I can opt for low tide, keeping the walk easy. Other times, I might choose the exhilaration of leaping over rocks, witnessing the power of incoming waves. This variation keeps me strong, my mind active, and my soul engaged in the journey of life.

Curious about what wisdom Celeste might offer on time's passage, I imagined her postcard from her travels:

Dear Brenda,

Have you noticed how the beach is never the same twice? Each tide erases and rewrites the shore's story, yet the beach itself endures. Your mother understands this—she's not fighting time's tide but dancing with it.

The fishermen you watched weren't measuring their lives by the clock but by the rhythms of sun and moon, wave and wind. They know that human time is but a small eddy in the great ocean of existence.

We don't own time—we're merely brief custodians of our small stretch of shoreline. The true art of living is deciding how to leave your mark before the tide returns.

Keep walking the shore,

Celeste

I picked up a small, perfectly formed sand dollar and turned it in my hand. Unlike the human-made clock with its rigid minutes and hours, nature's timepieces—the tides, the moon phases, the seasonal cycles—offer a more graceful measure of our days. Perhaps true wisdom lies in recognizing which timekeeper to follow in each season of life.

As these thoughts settled within me, I felt a profound shift in perspective. My hiking quest—now over 800 miles complete—wasn't really about the distance covered but about how I'd chosen to spend my allotted time. Each mile represented not just physical progress but a conscious decision to fill my days with wonder, challenge, and discovery.

The beach offered one final lesson as I prepared to leave. Near my turnaround point stood a piece of driftwood—once a mighty tree, now smoothed and silvered by time's passage. It hadn't been diminished by its journey but transformed, its essential nature revealed rather than destroyed by the elements. Perhaps that's what aging at its best can be—not a diminishment but a revelation of our true grain, our fundamental nature refined by time's tide. With this understanding, I was ready to bring this newfound peace with time to the remainder of my quest.

18.

POSSIBILITIES

Dates: September 15 – 21
Location: Oregon Coast, Southwest Oregon
Trails: Rockaway Beach, Cape Lookout Trail, Big Cedar Trail, Rogue River Trail, Bolt Mountain Trail
Miles Hiked in Week 18: 47.8
Total Miles Hiked: 882.3

MY WEEK BEGAN with what had become my ritual—a walk along the beach, just beyond Twin Rocks before turning back. On my return, a black garbage bag lying on the shore caught my eye. I faced a dilemma: pick it up and carry a wet, sandy bag for over a mile, or leave it, marring the beautiful beach scene. Could I really expect someone else to deal with it? With a sigh, I made my choice and picked it up.

This small act of environmental stewardship would lead to a more profound encounter. Just a bit further along, I spotted a bird, what looked to be a Marbled Murrelet, lying in the sand, clearly in distress. As I approached, it allowed me to touch it—a sign of its vulnerability. While its wings had dried, the underside was soaked. I imagined it had ventured too close to the water, exhausting itself in the struggle to reach shore.

Using the recently collected garbage bag, I gently scooped up the bird. My plan was to seek help from the county park staff, hoping they could connect me with a local bird rehabilitator. As I carried this fragile creature, I tried to provide warmth and comfort, one hand resting protectively on top. I wanted to convey, somehow, that I was trying my best to help.

"It's okay, my friend," I whispered, surprised by my own tenderness. "I've got you now."

The bird's rapid heartbeat against my palm was a poignant reminder of its fragility. As we reached the pavement, it lifted its head, meeting my gaze. I found myself instinctively soothing it, promising it would be alright. But nature had other plans. The heartbeat I'd been so acutely aware of suddenly stopped, and the warmth faded from the small body.

Tears rolled down my cheeks as I realized what had happened. Finding a quiet spot under a tree, I gently laid the bird to rest. Though the outcome wasn't what I'd hoped for, I found solace in knowing that this creature hadn't died alone on the cold sand. In its final moments, it had known care and comfort. Isn't that, after all, what any of us might hope for at the end?

This unexpected encounter left me contemplating the delicate balance of life and our role in the natural world. What had started as a simple act of picking up litter had become a profound reminder of our interconnectedness with all living things. The bird's passing stirred thoughts of mom—though her independence and spirit remained strong, the question of time hung in the air between us. I couldn't ignore this message from the universe—a reminder that presence matters more than distance.

In the bird's final moments, I'd witnessed something sacred—the importance of bearing witness, of simply being there. I couldn't shake the feeling that I needed to create those moments with my mother while I still could. As I looked forward to seeing her in two months, I carried both hope that her health would endure and a new understanding of what truly matters at life's thresholds.

On Monday, I drove to Cape Lookout and encountered what proved to be the muddiest trail of my entire journey. Wearing my oldest high-top hikers, I navigated stretches that resembled an intricate maze of mud interwoven with gnarled tree roots. The path was surprisingly crowded, with each passing hiker seemingly assessing the mud-caked condition of others' boots—a silent camaraderie in our shared challenge.

As I slogged forward, doubts crept in about whether any view could justify this messy ordeal. But when I finally reached the point, all hesitation vanished—the breathtaking panorama of powerful ocean waves crashing against the rugged cliff face transformed my muddy struggle into a worthwhile pilgrimage. The raw beauty of the coastline, with its untamed energy and sweeping vistas, made every slippery step a price worth paying.

I was in new territory and feeling adventurous, so after Cape Lookout, I drove without a mission. Heading south on the highway, I followed a sign for Sand Lake Recreation Area. This ability to take detours at will was one of my favorite aspects of travel, stumbling upon hidden gems almost by accident.

Sand Lake proved to be a pleasant surprise, offering a sensory puzzle that reminded me of those childhood picture books where you search for the thing that doesn't belong. As I strolled along the dune, the incongruity struck me the sound of crashing ocean waves accompanied a serene lake view. Crossing a shallow channel, I found myself on a narrow spit of sand, ocean waves roaring on one side, placid lake waters on the other. It was a surreal and captivating landscape.

Tuesday's weather, however, seemed tailor-made for curling up with a steaming cup of tea and a good book. Persistent drizzle and grey skies dominated the day. Still, I ventured out in the morning, driving a couple of miles to see the Big Cedar. The short boardwalk stroll led to an impressive giant cedar, its massive canopy offering some shelter from the rain. I walked the trail twice, enjoying the respite from the rain, before returning to the campground to add a few more steps to my daily count.

Wednesday marked my final day on the Oregon coast. I bid farewell with two walks along my now-familiar beach route and a final visit to the Tillamook creamery. While I'd enjoyed my coastal sojourn, I found myself eagerly anticipating sunnier days inland. The pull of the road was strong—I was ready to move again, to embrace new landscapes and challenges.

Thursday marked the beginning of another adventure, with a projected six-hour journey to Indian Mary Campground in Merlin, Oregon. Little did I know that my trusty RV GPS was about to lead me on a heart-pounding ride.

Following its instructions, I took the Wolf Creek exit, only to watch the two-lane road narrow ominously into a single, nerve-wracking lane. On one side, the river rushed by; on the other, a towering cliff loomed. The absence of oncoming traffic was my only saving grace—there was no place to pull over. A grim thought crossed my mind: with the Jeep in tow, backing up wasn't an option. I was committed to this white-knuckle ride, come what may.

"Celeste, what have I gotten myself into?" I muttered, gripping the steering wheel tighter.

The road, if you could call it that, had no shoulders to speak of. Instead, two-foot-deep ditches flanked the narrow strip of asphalt. The stakes were clear—one wrong move, one tire slipping into those ditches, and I'd be in a world of trouble.

This harrowing drive seemed to stretch on forever. My speed crawled to an average of 20 miles per hour, each mile a test of nerves and driving skill. At mile 17, my GPS cheerfully announced I had arrived at the campground. The only problem? I was smack in the middle of nowhere, not a campground in sight. As I crept past this phantom destination, the GPS blithely instructed me to continue for another 20 miles.

Reaching for my phone, hoping for a second opinion, I was met with another setback—no cell service. I was truly on my own, committed to this unexpected odyssey with no way to check an alternative route.

Finally, I crossed a bridge over the Rogue River, and the road began to widen. The reappearance of a painted center line felt like a small victory. When the campground sign finally came into view, relief washed over me.

At the check-in booth, I recounted my harrowing journey to the ranger. Her shocked exclamation, "You came that way!" confirmed what I'd begun to suspect: my GPS had chosen the worst route available.

My campground sat on the edge of the Wild Rogue Wilderness, a rugged expanse surrounding the Wild and Scenic Rogue River. True to its "wilderness" designation, cell service was non-existent, plunging me into a week of quiet solitude, free from the constant hum of phone, television, and internet. This digital detox led to occasional trips into town, where I'd seek out libraries or community parks to reconnect briefly with the online world.

On Friday morning, I set out for the Rogue River Trail, quite the contrast to the section of the Rogue that flows from Crater Lake. Without the familiar crutch of my AllTrails app or GPS, I stopped at a ranger station for directions. Without his help, I would never have found the trailhead, which required me to navigate a sharp left turn after the bridge and cautiously descend the steep, one-lane road to the boat launch.

The trail, stretching nearly forty miles through the Wild Rogue Wilderness, was typically a multi-day affair. My more modest goal was the Whiskey Creek cabin, an old gold miner's homestead that had earned its place on the National Register of Historic Places.

Setting out from the Grave Creek trailhead, I found myself on what I can only describe as a mountain goat trail, clinging precariously to the cliffside. Evidence of nature's power was everywhere—rockslides were the biggest threat, and in one particularly daunting section, wire mesh had been installed to secure the cliff face. Eventually, the narrow trail gave way to forested areas and even a few sandy beaches. A weathered sign marked the highest recorded level of the Rogue River in December 1964—an astonishing 52 feet above its summer level. Watching whitewater rafters navigate the rapids far below, I struggled to imagine the river swelling to such heights.

My solitary hike was punctuated by encounters with a group of six hikers and their guide. Our leap-frogging along the trail led to friendly exchanges and an introduction to the concept of "wiking"—a clever combination of afternoon hikes and evening wine tastings at wilderness lodges.

A brief detour to an open picnic area revealed a fascinating glimpse into wilderness safety measures—a bear box surrounded by an electric fence. The sight of a butterfly dancing on bear scat just outside the fence perimeter struck me as a poignant juxtaposition of nature's beauty and potential danger.

Finally reaching Whiskey Creek, I crossed an old wooden bridge to find the old cabin—a surprisingly large and well-preserved structure that exceeded my expectations. On my return journey, I again encountered the hiking group, politely declining their invitation to join them for lunch.

A chance exchange with some rafters on the river below led to an impromptu addition to my itinerary—I booked a seat on a Monday afternoon raft trip, eager to experience the river from a different perspective.

Saturday brought a change of scenery as I drove to nearby Grants Pass, seeking out Fish Hatchery Park and the trailhead to Bolt Mountain. As I began my ascent, an unexpected and lighthearted moment unfolded. An older couple, paused to capture their trail adventure on video, suddenly found themselves with an unintended guest star—me! In a burst of spontaneity, the gentleman turned his camera my way, leading to an impromptu and jovial interview. It was a reminder of the unexpected connections that can occur on the trail, even in the briefest of moments.

The hike up Bolt Mountain proved to be a moderate challenge, characterized by a steady incline winding through a series of switchbacks. Each turn brought new views and a sense of accomplishment as I climbed higher.

Reaching the summit, I found myself sharing the space with a group of four younger hikers, our paths converging at this pinnacle.

From this vantage point, the landscape unfurled before us, revealing its complex tapestry of natural beauty and human impact. A distant mountain, stripped bare by clearcutting, caught my eye. One of my summit companions offered an interesting insight—Oregon law mandates replanting of such areas within a few years. I couldn't help but remember the blemish of the clearcut hill in Washington, and hoped they had a similar law. This mountain jaunt highlighted the ongoing interplay between resource use and conservation efforts in these forests.

Descending Bolt Mountain, I felt drawn to explore more of Fish Hatchery Park. My wanderings led me to a spot overlooking the Applegate River, its waters glinting in the afternoon light. This peaceful scene provided a perfect counterpoint to the exertion of the climb, a moment to reflect on the varied experiences of the day. As I drove back to the campground, I carried with me not just the memory of the views from the summit, but also the warmth of shared laughter with strangers on the trail, and a deepened appreciation for the complex ecosystem—both natural and human—that I was traversing.

As I added my mileage for the week, I was pleased with the numbers. Yes, I had intended to slow down. But the Rogue River Wilderness and the sunshine called to me. I was having fun on the trail, and I hiked to my heart's content. Even with my scary travel day, I logged 47.8 miles, pushing my total to 882.3 miles. As I reflected on the week, I became aware of the small messages that appeared along the way—messages I might have missed had I not been paying attention.

POSSIBILITIES ARE THE GATEWAY TO JOY.

On that Oregon coast, late one evening, I looked up at the sky to discover a brilliant moon. It was the Hunter's Moon, also a supermoon, larger and brighter than usual because it hung closest to Earth. I captured this incredibly beautiful sight of the moon rising over the hills and shared it with my son. He replied with a photo of the same moon over the Grand Canyon. The sky was spectacular, and it felt magical, like something in the universe was connecting all of humanity together in one grand theatrical performance. Could this shared celestial moment be showing me that possibilities, like the moon, are visible from any vantage point?

That night, beneath that giant moon, brought restlessness and interrupted dreams. And then at 4 a.m., my future appeared! In that liminal space between sleeping and waking, when the mind is most receptive to subtle signals, I was finally quiet enough to hear what life had been trying to tell me.

My mind had been bouncing between memories of my father, reflections on my 1,000-mile quest, worries about mom, and visions of what lay ahead. Each time I'd close my eyes, another idea would spark. As the night wore on, a realization dawned—perhaps it was time to shake up my RVing routine. Five seasons on the road had gifted me with incredible experiences, crisscrossing the country and witnessing its myriad wonders. But now, a new thought emerged, electrifying in its simplicity: What if I could get paid to do what I love—hiking, kayaking, spending time in the great outdoors?

This spark—another small message I might have dismissed had I been too tired or distracted to listen—ignited a cascade of possibilities. Maybe it was time to view my life as an ongoing experiment. A summer job could be the perfect catalyst for change. It would ease my financial concerns, alleviating the pressure to generate entrepreneurial income. Plus, staying in one place for a season could offer the chance to build a sense of community. An active outdoor job would keep me in nature and in shape.

Energized, I reached out to my winter RV resort community, tapping into their wealth of experience with summer jobs. The responses were inspiring—one friend had spent a summer hiking to remote ruins in Bears Ears National Monument, occasionally assisting archaeologists. Another worked as an ATV guide near Bryce Canyon National Park. A posting for a hiking and kayaking guide outside Yellowstone National Park caught my eye. The prospects were thrilling.

But then, two nagging doubts crept in: Am I too old for this? Is this type of job "beneath" me? These questions led me back to my musings on personal freedom. Do I truly have freedom if I let my age, gender, education, or perceived social status limit my choices? As long as I can do the job, shouldn't that be all that matters? Why not pursue something purely for the joy of it?

And I realized that perhaps joy is really a mindset, an embrace of possibilities. When I lived in poverty, I saw only struggle ahead of me. But at this stage of life, I see possibilities. My life, my destiny is not laid out in front of me like a predetermined path. Instead, it is carved, shaped, and refined by me. And maybe, my own expectations of myself, my own snobbery, my perceptions of what is age-appropriate, have been an anchor to a place where

I don't want to stay. Have I chosen to slog through muddy trails when there was a simple shortcut available to me?

Deep down inside, I know there's a shortcut to joy. But to find that shortcut, I have to seriously unburden myself of the expectations that came with my degree, my salary, my career. It was time to return to the basics: the soft earth under my feet, the sound of birds singing in the morning, the glow of the sun as it rises over the canyons, the smell of a perfect bloom after a long rain. These basics don't require degrees. They only require an open heart and a soul of curiosity. And I bring that to the table.

The realization of my own snobbery and age bias caught me off guard. Having always taken pride in my rural working-class roots, I was surprised to find myself thinking that low-wage physical labor was somehow "beneath" me. This revelation was a much-needed wake-up call, a reminder to check my attitude at the door. Seeking wisdom, I imagined Celeste's response:

Dear Brenda,

Your age isn't a limit, it's a testament to the life you've lived and the wisdom you carry. The world tries to convince us that adventure has an expiration date, but nature knows better—some trees don't bear their first fruit until decades into their lives.

Don't let the world's expectations tell you what's "appropriate" for someone with your experience. The truth is, you're never too old to start anew, and there's no work "too small" if it feeds your spirit. Adventure isn't just for the young—it's for the bold, and you're as bold as they come.

What's beneath you is staying stuck in work that no longer brings joy. What's above you is the freedom to do what truly excites you, to connect with nature, and to guide others on their own journeys.

Choose a life that aligns with who you are, not who the world thinks you should be.

You've got this!

Celeste

Celeste's words calmed my thoughts, reminding me to live my life according to my own values and desires. As dawn broke, I felt a sense of excitement and possibility wash over me. This epiphany wasn't just about finding a new job; it was about embracing adventure and aligning my life more closely with my true passions. The path ahead was uncertain, but it sparkled with promise.

This quest has crystallized a crucial realization: from here on out, my health must be my top priority. I'm still operating with all my original parts, and these hikes have not only strengthened me physically but deepened my appreciation for what my body can do. These hikes have shown me that my physical capabilities open doors to possibilities I might otherwise miss. I've always lived by the mantra, "do it while you can, because you might never get another chance." Now, more than ever, that philosophy resonates.

The challenge now is to regain true freedom in my life and return to the boldness I once embraced. It's about not giving a damn about what others think and instead focusing on what truly fulfills me. This shift in perspective isn't just about career choices; it's about reclaiming the authenticity of my experiences and the diversity of my capabilities.

As I approach the 900-mile mark next week, I'm filled with a sense of accomplishment and anticipation. The prospect of becoming a guide—of sharing my passion for nature and adventure with others—feels like a natural evolution. It's a way to combine my physical abilities, my love for the outdoors, and the wisdom I've accumulated over six decades of life. And isn't that the essence of aging well? Not retreating from life, but finding new ways to engage with it fully, discovering new possibilities at every turn?

Even that brief, lighthearted moment with the older couple filming their hike on Bolt Mountain had been a small message worth noting. Their joy, their playfulness in documenting their adventure, their spontaneous inclusion of a stranger in their narrative—it reminded me that connections can happen anywhere, at any age, if we remain open to them. Perhaps the outdoor work I was contemplating would offer not just physical engagement but rich human connections as well.

The trail ahead is unknown, but one thing is certain: I'm ready to embrace whatever challenges and joys it may bring, with an open heart and the courage to keep pushing boundaries. When I began this journey, I was focused on counting miles, checking off trails, and proving something to myself. Now, as I approach the finish line, I've learned that possibilities are indeed the gateway to joy—and they appear not when we're rigidly following our plans but when we're quiet enough to listen for life's subtle messages, attentive enough to notice the unexpected signs along the way, and brave enough to follow where they lead.

In the end, I realized that the most profound joy doesn't come from reaching a destination but from recognizing the infinite possibilities that each new day brings. Mom understands this instinctively, finding delight in simple moments despite her illness. Those mountains I've climbed, those trails I've conquered—they've shown me landscapes I'd never have seen otherwise. But the greatest vista they've revealed is the expansive horizon of possibility that spreads before me now, unlimited by age, unconstrained by convention, waiting only for my courage to explore it. Tomorrow, I'll step onto another trail, not just to add miles, but to discover what new possibilities await.

19.

INTO THE WILD

Dates: September 22 – 28
Location: Southwest Oregon, Central California
Trails: Rogue River Trail, Cathedral Hills Trail
Miles Hiked in Week 19: 47.2
Total Miles Hiked: 929.5

AFTER TWO DAYS of strenuous hiking, Sunday offered a welcome respite with a casual morning and evening strolls around the campground. As dusk settled, I took in the sight of a turkey perched regally on a yurt's deck railing, orange safety netting erected nearby. I watched, amused, as the turkey leapt off its perch, then called to its companions seemingly trapped on the other side of the netting. What followed was a comical turkey spectacle—each bird taking a running start to fly over the barrier, joining their alpha. Their raucous gobbling shattered the evening's tranquility before they continued their journey. "Nature's comedy show," I smiled to myself. Such moments of witnessing nature's quirks and wildlife's antics are joys I hope to never take for granted.

Monday brought the excitement of rafting day. With the season winding down and excursions limited to afternoons, I spent the morning walking loops around the campground before heading to the outfitter's base. The day's 90-degree high made me grateful to be on the water. Once on the river, I enjoyed a mostly serene journey punctuated by a few thrilling moments navigating Class 2 and 3 rapids. The cool spray on my face as we crashed through the whitecaps awakened every sense. While I'd hoped for a display of autumn colors, the trees had yet to turn.

Invigorated by the adventure, I capped off the day with more campground loops and a call to mom. I told her about the day's rafting trip and the turkeys from the night before. But I skipped sharing tales of the treacherous drive to the campground. Mom worried about me, out on the road alone, and I made a vow to reassure her of my safety, at every opportunity. This selective sharing felt like its own form of care—protecting her from unnecessary worry while still maintaining our connection. "You sound happy," she'd said, and I realized I truly was.

Tuesday saw me return to the Rogue River Trail, eager to discover what lay beyond Whiskey Creek cabin. The answer: more exceptional beauty. I paused at the creek to record the melodious sound of water tumbling over rocks. "I need to remember this," I whispered to myself, closing my eyes to imprint the moment in memory. My journey culminated at a perfect turnaround point—a log perched atop a cliff overlooking the river. Recalling the painted rock's message to "find stillness," I savored every minute on my lofty perch, feeling profound gratitude for all life had given me. As evening approached, I once again found myself at the boat launch, capturing another colorful sunset.

Wednesday, my final day in Oregon, took me to Grants Pass to explore Cathedral Hill's trails. The autumn day was picture-perfect for hiking. Cathedral Hills itself proved a wild maze of trails, necessitating frequent consultations with my AllTrails app. The peaks, while promising, were frustratingly ringed with "No Trespassing—Private Property" signs, secreting panoramic mountain views from public eyes. This disappointing final hike echoed the letdown of my last Washington trek, a bittersweet end to my Oregon adventures.

Despite this anticlimactic finish, my time on the Rogue River had been truly magical. From serene moments of stillness to thrilling rapids, from comical turkey antics to breathtaking sunsets, the river had shown me its many faces. As I prepared to leave Oregon, I carried with me a deepened appreciation for the wild beauty of the Rogue and the myriad ways it had enriched my journey.

On Thursday morning I took a final, mindful loop around the campground before hitting the road. I silently thanked Oregon for all it had given me as I pointed my rig south. By afternoon, I'd arrived at the RV resort in Corning—the same spot where I'd stayed on my northward journey, and where Coco had staged her grand escape. This familiar stop offered a chance to catch up on laundry and restock supplies.

Friday's destination was Horseshoe Bend Recreation Area on Lake McClure, but my GPS had other ideas, leading me to Lake McClure Recreation Area instead. Upon arrival, I learned Horseshoe Bend was another 30-minute drive away.

"Not again," I muttered, recalling my harrowing GPS misadventure from the previous week. I glanced at the sky, imagining Celeste looking down at me, whispering words of assurance, "You'll be just fine!"

As if I hadn't endured enough white-knuckle driving, I found myself navigating a narrow, winding road following the booth attendant's directions. The road's fresh, almost glowing yellow stripes belied its true nature—a roller coaster of uneven pavement that had my rig swaying alarmingly. At one point, steering became so difficult I feared a blown tire, but an inspection revealed the culprit was simply the road's treacherous condition.

When the GPS announced I'd reached the campground, all I could see was an unmarked dirt road. Wary of another misdirection, I continued until I found a wide turnout to consult my phone's map. Confirming the location, I made a U-turn and cautiously took the dirt road. A sign visible only from this direction confirmed I was in the right place. Later, I learned from the ranger that someone had stolen both the campground and curve signs—an explanation that did little to soothe my frayed nerves.

I was in for another California scorcher. While out exploring on Saturday, I discovered Coulterville's Coyotefest was in full swing. I caught the tail end of the parade—local posse members waving from horseback, leashed goats strolling with their owners, 4H kids tossing candy, and a goofy pirate swinging on a float. This small-town celebration was a heartwarming reminder of simpler times. I indulged in a meal and browsed the craft booths, soaking in the community atmosphere.

My explorations continued with a drive to gauge the distance to Yosemite National Park, hoping to revisit one of my favorite spots for a hike or two if temperatures permitted. A stop in Groveland yielded another stroke of luck—

a library book sale. True to my promise to read more and surf less, I left with four books.

As the week drew to a close, my primary concern shifted to the impending triple-digit temperatures forecast for the coming days. It felt like déjà vu, reminiscent of my sweltering stay in Coarsegold on my northward journey. Suddenly, I was grateful for the "extra" miles I'd accumulated on my quest, providing a buffer to accommodate a heat wave-induced slowdown.

On Saturday night, I tallied the week's miles. I had some big hikes, with 10.1 miles on the Rogue River Trail on Tuesday and another 11.3 miles on Wednesday's Cathedral Hills Trail. While I was intent on slowing down, those hikes were fun, and even easy. I could not have imagined an 11-mile hike being "easy" when I first set out in May. But here I was, with another solid week, marked by 47.2 miles. I had reached 929.5 miles, almost an unbelievable feat. As I reflected on this progress, a sense of quiet accomplishment washed over me.

JOY IS REBELLIOUS.

Initially, the lack of cell service at Indian Mary Campground irked me. Connectivity had always been high on my priority list when selecting campsites. But surrounded by nature, cut off from digital ties, I found myself slipping into a lifestyle that somehow expanded time itself. In this disconnected wilderness, I discovered something powerful: joy is an act of rebellion.

In a world where the 24-hour news cycle, social media algorithms, and political machinery profit from our anxiety and outrage, choosing joy becomes a radical stance. By unplugging, I was resisting the constant pull to remain angry, afraid, and divided.

My final Oregon hike brought this lesson into sharp focus. At the Cathedral Hills trailhead, a house festooned with political signs—including one proudly proclaiming "Voting for a Felon"—haunted my thoughts for miles. It transported me back to a college project on 1930s American media, where I'd tracked the dehumanizing rhetoric that preceded Nazi atrocities. Hannah Arendt's writings on the "banality of evil" echoed in my mind.

The parallels disturbed me deeply. Here we stand at the crossroads of American democracy, airwaves filled with divisive language that left me feeling both tormented and powerless. Then I realized: allowing these thoughts to dominate my mind wasn't just stealing my joy—it was surrendering to exactly what those who profit from division want. They thrive when we're exhausted and bitter because that's when we're easiest to manipulate.

The wilderness offered a solution: compartmentalization. Without constant connectivity, I'd learned to schedule my online time. Perhaps I could apply the same principle to politics—limit my exposure, then disconnect and return to presence?

These unplugged days helped answer that perennial question: "Where did the time go?" In the Rogue Wilderness, with hours no longer vanishing into political rabbit holes, days stretched longer and my mood brightened. It wasn't coincidence. I vowed to maintain this boundary between necessary awareness and destructive obsession. This tech detox had shown me the value of conscious time management and rediscovering forgotten pleasures, like reading a fast-paced novel.

At Horseshoe Bend, my commitment was immediately tested by new neighbors, the "Whiskey Bandits," who rolled in with a giant political flag fluttering defiantly from their truck. The sight triggered an immediate flash of anger that tightened my chest. But in that moment, I caught myself at the crossroads of reaction versus response. I took a deep breath and made a conscious choice: their provocative display might occupy physical space beside me, but I would not surrender my internal landscape to their hostility. Some battles aren't worth fighting, and some victories come not from confrontation but from refusing to engage in someone else's war.

Joy, I was learning, is not passive acceptance or willful ignorance. It's a declaration that while I care deeply about our world's problems, I refuse to be consumed by them. Maintaining my inner light makes me stronger, clearer, and more effective in whatever battles need fighting. A burned-out, bitter activist helps no one. A joyful, centered person who takes meaningful action without losing herself—that's true rebellion.

Still, I felt caught between two worlds—that hard road of relentless technological advancement and increasing social divisiveness, and the soft road of nature and respect for all of Earth's creatures. How could I bridge this divide? How could I maintain my connection to simplicity while still engaging with the world as it is? In search of guidance, I imagined penning a letter to Celeste, my wise friend and mentor, and awaiting her response on one of her postcards:

Dear Brenda,

We live in a time when division and anger are the currency of power. The more exhausted, fearful, and bitter we become, the easier we are to control. That's why your choice to unplug was a small but powerful act of rebellion.

Joy isn't a luxury or an indulgence. It's a lifeline, a compass that keeps you oriented toward what truly matters when the world tries to pull you into its frenzy. It's the strength to care without drowning, to fight without becoming what you oppose.

True freedom isn't found in escaping the world's problems, but in refusing to let them define you. That's the rebellion—to remain whole and joyful in a system designed to fragment and embitter.

With fierce joy,

Celeste

Celeste's words reminded me that joy isn't just a feeling—it's a stance, a position, a way of engaging with the world that refuses to surrender to cynicism and despair. I realized that my choice to protect my joy wasn't selfish; it was necessary for sustainable engagement with the very issues I cared about.

Perhaps the week's most profound revelation was the reclaiming of time itself. In the Rogue Wilderness, stripped of constant connectivity, I'd rediscovered the richness of uncluttered hours and joy's rebellious power. I'd glimpsed how to live without surrendering my emotional wellbeing to forces that profit from my distress.

Magical things seem to happen when I am intentional with my time. Rather than letting hours dissolve in mindless scrolling or reactive outrage, I could consciously choose how to spend each moment, creating boundaries around technology and news consumption while protecting space for nature walks, reading, and quiet reflection. These weren't just pleasant activities but small sanctuaries of resistance—defiant pockets of meaning in a culture that profits from our distraction and division.

I stood in an "in-between" space—between the woman who started this quest and the one I was becoming, between the connected world I'd left and the intentional life I was crafting, between counting miles and savoring moments. "Who are you becoming?" I asked myself as sunset painted Lake

McClure in brilliant hues. This threshold wasn't uncomfortable terrain to hurry through but a gift—the rare chance to consciously choose who I wanted to be. The discomfort was merely evolution's growing pain.

The looming California heat wave would be manageable. The extra miles I'd accumulated provided a buffer, allowing me to ease my pace without jeopardizing my goal—a gift from my past self to my future self, a tangible reminder of preparation's value.

Settling into my campsite, watching another sunset mark the week's close, gratitude washed over me. Not just for miles covered, but for insights gained, simplicity rediscovered, and presence restored. My journey nearly complete, I was unlocking the keys to joy. With just over 70 miles remaining, the finish line within sight, I already had much of what I needed—a path back to myself and the recognition that in a world profiting from division and despair, choosing joy is perhaps the most rebellious act of all. The final miles would be a celebration, not a race. Whatever lessons they held, I would meet them with an open heart, a clear mind, and a rebellious spirit.

20.

THE WEEK OF RECKONING

Dates: September 29 – October 5
Location: Central California
Trails: Preston Falls Trail
Miles Hiked in Week 20: 41.1
Total Miles Hiked: 970.6

THERE'S A PECULIAR tension that emerges when you stand at the threshold of completion. As I was closing in on that magical 1,000-mile mark, I found myself in that strange psychological territory where success felt inevitable yet still not quite mine to claim. Like a marathon runner glimpsing the finish line banner in the distance, I could sense the end of this journey approaching, feel its gravitational pull, even as the final miles still demanded their due.

Week 20 arrived with triple-digit heat that forced me to confront a fundamental question: How would I navigate this final stretch? Would I push through in a determined sprint to the end, or would I honor the promise I'd made to myself to slow down and savor these concluding miles?

Sunday morning found me driving to the Preston Falls trailhead in Stanislaus National Forest, near Yosemite's west entrance. My GPS guided me along a winding road with stomach-dropping views, eventually leading to the Hetch Hetchy Reservoir—San Francisco Bay Area's lifeline, delivering water to millions some 167 miles away. The engineering marvel seemed to echo my own journey—a long, carefully constructed path to bring something essential from source to destination.

I'd timed my start early, hoping to dodge the day's impending heat. The Tuolumne River provided a constant soundtrack to my trek, and I paused occasionally to capture its wild beauty. All these months of trail experience had taught me to stay alert for hazards—both visible ones like the reported poison oak, and those that might catch you unaware.

Then, at mile 933, my quest nearly met its dramatic end. Climbing a rocky hill, a sound that every hiker dreads pierced the morning air—the unmistakable rattle of a snake's warning. From my peripheral vision, I caught movement barely two feet away. Pure instinct took over; I didn't dare turn my head to look. Instead, I discovered what felt like rocket boosters in my hiking boots, my acceleration from casual walk to escape velocity nothing short of impressive.

"Oh my god," I gasped, once I was safely up the trail. I smiled upward at the sky, imagining Celeste looking down, "that was a close one, my friend," I admonished.

Heart pounding, adrenaline surging, I continued forward, my mind racing with the sobering thought—how close had I come to ending my quest, perhaps even my life, at mile 933? I thought fleetingly of my mother waiting for my Thanksgiving visit. How devastated she would be if I never made it.

The rattlesnake encounter created a stark moment of perspective. After nearly a thousand miles, hundreds of hours on countless trails across multiple states, my journey could have ended in an instant. Not with the triumphant celebration I'd imagined, but with a single misplaced step. The universe had just delivered a powerful reminder: we never fully control our journeys, only how we respond to what we encounter along the way.

Pressing on with heightened vigilance, I climbed around fallen trees and through tall grass, constantly scanning for more surprises. The trail eventually led to a large rock overlooking Preston Falls—a perfect spot to pause and process my close encounter. As I sat enjoying my trail snack of almonds, cranberries, and cheese under crystal blue skies, the waterfall's constant motion seemed to mirror my own journey—sometimes rushing headlong over obstacles, sometimes finding the path of least resistance, but always, always moving forward.

The return journey loomed with a new weight of anticipation. Knowing I'd have to pass the snake's territory again, I employed every trick in my hiking arsenal. My trekking poles became impromptu percussion instruments as I banged them together, sending advance warning to any nearby creatures. I even broke into song, improvising lyrics: "In the forest, the lovely forest, the rattler sleeps tonight..." The combination of noise and nervous energy carried me through without further encounters, though my adrenaline had long since faded.

After my rattlesnake encounter, I called mom. Our conversation was both ordinary and precious—she talked about her doctor's visits and her lunch with "the girls," unaware of how close I'd come to danger. I didn't mention the rattler, or how the thought of her had flashed through my mind in that moment of peril. Her voice, slightly frailer than the month before, reminded me that some journeys—like her battle with cancer—required a different kind of courage than facing wilderness trails. Our upcoming time together now felt even more important, more sacred.

As September yielded to October, I discovered one of autumn's sweetest gifts—near-empty campgrounds. With just one or two other RVers sharing the space, I found myself immersed in nature's intimate moments. Coyotes serenaded the setting sun, while mornings brought spectacular sunrises that transformed Lake McClure into a shimmering mirror. A hawk kept watch from its power line perch as deer families wandered the woods below, and a solitary heron stood sentinel at the water's edge.

The lake's low water level revealed temporary "islands"—secret topographies that would vanish once the reservoir filled again. I couldn't help but see this as another metaphor for my journey. My quest had revealed aspects of myself that had been submerged for years—strengths, joys, capacities for wonder that had been hidden beneath the high-water mark of my busy life. Would they remain visible once I returned to "normal" routines? Or would they submerge again, waiting for the next drought of certainty to reveal them?

On Wednesday afternoon, the metaphorical became literal when I suddenly found myself without power. After checking circuits and the pedestal, I discovered the entire campground was quiet. A series of increasingly frustrated phone calls finally revealed a power company outage. I fired up my generator to keep the air conditioning running, grateful when power was eventually restored.

But that night, as I drifted off to sleep, the familiar hum of electricity disappeared again. Too weary to investigate with flashlight in hand, I left the mystery for morning. Daylight brought a systematic check of the usual suspects—circuit breaker, surge protector, pedestal power. I turned to my Winnebago Aspect Facebook group for help, leading me to discover a burned-out transfer switch fuse.

What followed was a masterclass in the art of waiting. The campground's remote location worked against me—one RV mechanic quoted $600 just for the trip! Finally, I found "Jake," who promised a reasonable travel fee and 10 a.m. arrival. As 10 a.m. became 11, then noon, I ran the engine to keep the cats cool. When the temperature inside hit 80 degrees and the gas gauge dipped ominously low, it was time for Plan B.

I harnessed Izzy and Coco and moved them to the covered pavilion, where we sat through the scorching afternoon—the cats sprawled on cool concrete while I paced. Jake finally arrived at 4:30, apologizing for truck troubles before successfully bypassing the transfer switch.

After restoring power to my rig, I was surprised when night fell not with relief but with a deep, unexpected melancholy. I stood outside under a star-scattered sky, listening to coyotes harmonize in the distance, and felt the first real pangs of impending loss. For almost five months, this quest had given me purpose, structure, challenge. It had transformed me from someone seeking meaning into someone actively creating it with each step. What would happen when it ended?

On Friday, I was glad to get back on the road, and relieved to have an uncomplicated drive to Codorniz Campground at Eastman Lake, a beautiful but isolated spot nestled in California's rolling golden hills. Though short in distance, the serpentine mountain roads made the drive somewhat challenging. My jerry-rigged electrical system caused occasional worry, especially with temperatures still hovering around 100 degrees. Like my previous stop, the campground stood largely empty—a mixed blessing of solitude and limited human contact.

After a restless night, I greeted Saturday's sunrise outside my rig. It marked the sixth consecutive day of triple-digit heat, but those "extra" miles banked in previous months gave me permission to take a leisurely pace on the Lakeside Trail. As I hiked that morning, a clarity emerged that had been building all week.

The trail ahead wound through rocky terrain and down into shadowed ravines, but I could see just enough of the path to trust my next steps. Similarly, while I couldn't yet see exactly what awaited me after mile 1,000, I knew I could trust the person this journey had shaped me into.

The rattlesnake had taught me respect without paralyzing fear. The power outage had reminded me that problems have solutions, even when they're not immediate or obvious. The heat had demonstrated that adaptation isn't defeat but wisdom. These weren't just isolated lessons but a curriculum preparing me for whatever came next.

At 970.6 miles, with 41.1 added this week despite the challenges, I stood at the edge of completion—close enough to see the finish line, yet still with miles to cover. I was no longer the same person who set out to walk 1,000 miles. That woman had needed to prove something to herself. This woman, tested by rattlesnakes and heat waves, strengthened by solitude and challenge, had nothing left to prove—only more adventures to embrace.

JOY IS FORGED IN ADVERSITY AND RESILIENCE.

As the week's challenges piled up—first the snake, then the power problems, then the unrelenting heat—I had experienced moments of genuine despair. Would anything go right? Would this final stretch of my journey be nothing but a series of trials to endure? Yet here I stood, having navigated it all, having found solutions or adaptations for each difficulty. The joy I felt now wasn't despite these challenges but because of them—a hard-earned satisfaction that no easy path could have provided.

This realization shifted my understanding of joy itself. I had often thought of joy as something found in beautiful moments or pleasant experiences—the perfect sunset, the achievement of a goal, the companionship of friends. And certainly, those moments bring their own kind of happiness. But this week had revealed a deeper, more durable kind of joy—one not dependent on favorable circumstances but forged precisely in their absence.

It reminded me of the growth rings in trees. In favorable years, trees grow quickly, creating wider, softer rings. But it's the narrow rings, formed during years of drought and hardship, that give the tree its true strength and character. Perhaps joy works in a similar way—not developing most fully in easy times but in moments of challenge, when we must dig deeper, reach further, and discover resources within ourselves we never knew existed.

I thought of my mother's battle with cancer—certainly not a journey she would have chosen, but one that was revealing her remarkable strength and grace. Our phone call after my rattlesnake encounter had carried a deeper resonance precisely because we were both navigating difficult terrain, both discovering resilience we might never have known in easier circumstances.

This understanding changed how I viewed not just this week's trials but the entire journey. The steep climbs that had left me gasping for breath, the wrong turns that had added miles to my day, the white-knuckled drives that had tested my determination—these weren't unfortunate detours from the "real" journey but essential components of it. They were the fire and hammer that had forged something valuable within me.

As I considered the approaching completion of my thousand-mile quest, I realized that its value lay not in the achievement itself but in the person who had been shaped by its challenges. Had I somehow been able to complete these miles without difficulty, without moments that tested my limits, the achievement would have been hollow—a number without meaning, a distance without transformation.

Standing on the shore of Eastman Lake as the day's heat finally began to wane, I imagined what wisdom Celeste might offer on her next postcard:

Dear Brenda,

The most valuable things are rarely created in comfort. Gold must be melted to be purified, steel must be heated and hammered to gain its strength. Joy, too, reaches its fullest expression not in ease but in challenge overcome.

You're discovering what mountaineers, explorers, and seekers have always known: the most meaningful journeys aren't the easiest ones. The view is sweetest from peaks that demand your everything to summit. The joy is deepest when it's been earned through struggle.

The joy you feel now has been forged in every difficulty, every decision, every moment you chose to continue when stopping would have been easier.

That's a joy no one can take from you because you've earned it step by difficult step.

Rooted in resilience with you,

Celeste

As night fell, I sat outside my rig, watching the first stars appear. The day's heat still radiated from the earth, but a slight breeze had begun to stir, offering the promise of eventual relief. I thought about the challenges of this week—not with regret but with a strange sense of appreciation. Without the rattlesnake, I might not have felt the fierce surge of survival instinct that reminded me how much I valued my life. Without the power crisis, I might not have discovered the depths of my resourcefulness and patience. Without the heat, I might not have learned how much stronger I had become over these months of hiking

Tomorrow would bring a new week, and with it, the final miles of my journey. But tonight, I sat with the understanding that whatever challenges those miles might bring, they wouldn't diminish the experience but enhance it. Like a blacksmith who knows the purpose of the fire, I could now face difficulties with the awareness that they weren't just obstacles but essential elements in forging something valuable.

With less than 30 miles remaining, I was ready—not just to finish the journey but to embrace whatever challenges the final miles might bring, knowing that each one would only strengthen the joy being forged within me.

21.

THE FINISH LINE

Dates: October 6 – 12
Location: Central California
Trails: Eastman Lake Trail
Miles Hiked in Week 20: 50.9
Total Miles Hiked: 1021.5

I COULD HARDLY believe it—my 1,000-mile quest was entering its final week. The forecast showed more triple-digit temperatures ahead, but the cool mornings gave me confidence I could dodge the worst of the heat. Sunday's sunrise found me pushing through tall grass near my campsite to reach the Eastman Lake trail. The path led behind the campground to the main road which, given the park's remote location in central California's golden hills, stood deserted. The silence was profound, broken only by the rhythmic crunch of my boots on the dirt path and the occasional call of a hawk circling overhead.

After passing park headquarters and the observation area, my AllTrails map guided me beyond an "Authorized Vehicles Only" sign to an unexpected treat—Buchanan Dam. Crossing the massive structure, I felt a surge of awe at human engineering juxtaposed against nature's wild beauty. I followed a narrow trail bordered by oat grass, then some paved roads, finally wandering across an open field to an old windmill before turning back. I made it to the campground before the day's 100-degree heat could catch up with me, logging a satisfying 8.1 miles.

"Just over 20 miles to go," I whispered to myself, still amazed that what had once seemed like an impossible goal now stood within reach. That evening, I called my mother to share my progress. Despite all she was enduring, her enthusiasm was undimmed. "I always knew you'd do it," she said with quiet confidence. "You've never been one to give up." Her pride in me filled me with a renewed determination to finish strong. My achievement felt like a gift I could share with her—proof that her lifelong belief in me had borne fruit.

Monday's adventure began at dawn's first light, this time heading in the opposite direction with Raymond Bridge, 4.5 miles away, as my destination. Saturday's hike had shown me the rugged nature of this section, but I felt prepared. The morning air carried a hint of autumn crispness that would soon surrender to the day's heat. Resting at the bridge, I faced a pivotal decision: turn back for a 9-mile day, or complete the lake loop for what AllTrails promised would be 11.7 miles.

"I've come this far," I thought, surveying the tranquil water and the path ahead. "What's another couple of miles?"

The previous day's easy dam crossing boosted my confidence about the return trek, and knowing the ranger station lay along my route provided an extra sense of security—a potential water stop or even a ride if needed. Still energized from the shady side of the lake, I added electrolytes to my water and committed to the loop.

The decision seemed sound until I encountered an unexpected obstacle—a 'No Trespassing' sign, locked gate, and barbed wire fence marking a conservation area. My app showed no alternate route, and backtracking would add miles to my trek in the hot sun, making it potentially dangerous. After wrestling with the dilemma, I made what I felt to be the safest choice—carefully stepping over the fence to follow a trail through pastureland, navigating past a herd of cattle before climbing another fence back onto public land.

Finally, the familiar windmill came into view, signaling my return to known territory. The sight filled me with relief, but I was beginning to recognize the telltale signs of heat stress in my body.

As temperatures climbed, my pace slowed dramatically. A passing park ranger's wave gave me false confidence as I crossed the dam. The home stretch—a downhill road walk and trail back to the campground—seemed deceptively manageable. Then, without warning, heat exhaustion struck. Nausea and a racing heart forced me to stop, seeking refuge in patches of shade. I found myself counting steps between shade spots, no longer caring about finding rocks or logs to sit on—the ground itself became my rest stop. This desperate shade-to-shade strategy repeated five or six times before I finally reached my air-conditioned RV.

The thermometer read 95 degrees, but the real surprise came when I checked my mileage—the AllTrails 11.7-mile route had actually been 12.6 miles. That final, unexpected mile had nearly been my undoing. As relief washed over me, water in hand on my sofa, I realized how quickly heat stroke had sneaked up on me. By the time I recognized the warning signs, I was already in trouble. My decision to hike the loop had almost cost me dearly on this, the final week of my quest.

Tuesday brought a negligible respite from the heat—98 degrees instead of triple digits. Still sobered by the previous day's close call, I opted for a gentle walk to the boat launch and back. Evening found me strolling through the nearly deserted campground, where I spotted a bobcat in the fading light, a sight that would become a cherished ritual over the next two evenings. The bobcat's calm presence reminded me that I was still just a visitor in this landscape, privileged to witness its natural rhythms.

Wednesday dawned with electric anticipation—just 3.5 miles stood between me and the magical 1,000-mile mark. The knowledge that today would be the day filled me with a mixture of excitement and disbelief. Had I really walked nearly a thousand miles since that first step in May? The morning air seemed charged with possibility as I prepared for what would be the most significant hike of my journey.

I set out across the dam, searching for the perfect backdrop to commemorate this momentous achievement. The rising sun cast long shadows across the path, and I felt lighter with each step, as if five months of accumulated determination was propelling me forward. Every landmark along the way seemed to take on special significance—the lone oak tree, the curve in the shoreline, the distant mountains framing the landscape. These weren't just features on a trail anymore; they were witnesses to my milestone.

As I climbed a hill at mile 999, a roadrunner darted across my path, then leaped onto a boulder to study me, as if offering advance congratulations.

"Well, hello there!" I called out, delighted by this unexpected companionship at such a significant moment.

Many Native American tribes view roadrunners as harbingers of good fortune, and the timing of this encounter felt deeply significant. The bird cocked its head, its bright eyes seeming to acknowledge what was about to happen, before darting away into the brush.

A few small loops brought me to a scenic overlook, where I watched my app tick over to the milestone I'd dreamed of for months: Mile 1,000! The journey that began on May 19 had reached its culmination on October 9, 144 days of determination, discovery, and growth.

"I did it! A THOUSAND MILES!" I shouted into the open air, startling a flock of birds from a nearby tree. I'd spent weeks wondering how this moment would feel. Would it seem anticlimactic, or would I be overwhelmed with emotion? Standing there beneath the vast blue sky, gazing out over the tranquil lake, the answer crystallized in a rush of pure, unadulterated joy. I had done it! I reached my arms skyward in triumph, spinning in a small circle, laughing out loud at the sheer exhilaration of the moment.

I'd walked the equivalent distance from San Francisco to Seattle—across mountains and valleys, through forests and deserts, in sunshine and rain. My body, nearly 61 years old, had carried me every step of the way.

I took photos to commemorate the milestone, trying to capture the radiance I felt inside. But how could a simple image convey the millions of steps, the countless challenges, the moments of doubt and perseverance that had brought me here? This wasn't just about reaching a number—it was about proving to myself that I could set an audacious goal and see it through, one step at a time.

As I made my way back to the campground, I felt as though I was floating rather than walking. The milestone behind me, I now had the freedom to simply enjoy the journey without the pressure of the goal. For the first time in months, I walked without calculating distances or planning routes to meet my daily quota. I was simply present, savoring the feeling of the earth beneath my feet and the knowledge that I had accomplished something remarkable.

As the week unfolded, a subtle but profound shift occurred—being released from that rigid 6.5-mile daily hiking goal felt like stepping into a gentler way of being. Though I still covered an average of six miles each day, I walked at my own pace, letting my body, not my app, guide the way. I finished the week with a hefty 50.9 miles, bringing my total to 1021.5 miles.

After some quick calculations, I recorded my final statistics. I had hiked 1003.2 miles in 144 days, for an average of 7 miles per day. I had accomplished my goal, with weeks to spare. My most ambitious trek stretched 12.6 miles—that fateful Eastman Lake loop where heat stroke stalked my final steps. At the other end of the spectrum lay a mere 6/10 of a mile in mid-July, when summer storms and bone-deep weariness kept me nestled in my rig. Through it all, I met or exceeded my 6.5-mile daily goal on 100 of those 144 days, each step a testament to perseverance.

I was proud of myself, but what filled me with even greater satisfaction was the profound personal growth I'd experienced since first lacing up my hiking boots all those months ago. The woman who had begun this journey—uncertain, seeking purpose, questioning her path—had been transformed. With each mile, I had shed limiting beliefs and discovered new reserves of strength, resilience, and clarity about what truly mattered.

And now, the road was calling me homeward. I shortened my stay by a day, heading to the RV resort in Bakersfield where I spent a peaceful day restoring order—washing away trail dust from clothes and giving my "Goldie 17" rig the thorough cleaning it deserved. On October 14, I guided my RV through familiar gates and settled into my winter home. The journey had come full circle, bringing me back to where the idea had first taken root. But I returned transformed, carrying within me not just memories of a thousand miles, but the wisdom and strength those miles had instilled.

TRUE JOY COMES FROM CROSSING YOUR OWN FINISH LINE.

Standing at mile 1,000, with a roadrunner as my only witness, I understood something profound about joy that all my previous miles had been preparing me to grasp. True joy doesn't come from crossing someone else's finish line or reaching a milestone others have established. It emerges when you define your own challenge, walk your own path, and recognize the moment of completion not as the world might see it, but as your heart knows it to be.

The joy that surged through me at that moment was unlike anything I'd experienced before—a perfect alchemy of pride, relief, wonder, and something deeper for which I had no name. This wasn't the fleeting happiness of a purchase or the social satisfaction of recognition. This was a soul-deep exultation born from the knowledge that I had committed to something difficult, persisted through doubt and challenge, and emerged triumphant through my own determination.

Unlike manufactured finish lines—the promotions and accolades, the material acquisitions, the social media milestones that society uses to measure success—this one carried the unmistakable resonance of authenticity. I hadn't walked a thousand miles to impress anyone or to check a box on some culturally prescribed list of achievements. I had walked them for myself, to prove something to myself, to discover something about myself that could only be revealed through the steady accumulation of miles and experiences.

What made this joy so complete, so transformative, was that it couldn't be diminished by anyone else's opinion or measured against anyone else's standard. No one could take it from me because no one had given it to me. I had earned it step by step, through gloomy days and heat waves, through doubt and determination. It was mine in a way that few things in life truly are.

This realization cast new light on the joy I'd experienced throughout my journey. Those moments of elation atop difficult climbs, of wonder at unexpected vistas, of connection with strangers on the trail—they had all been authentic because they had occurred on a path I had chosen for myself. Even the hardships—the rattlesnake encounter, the storms that had driven me to shelter, the heat exhaustion I'd battled just days ago—had contributed to this culminating joy because they had been part of my path, not obstacles on a journey someone else had prescribed.

As I gazed out over the tranquil waters of Eastman Lake, I realized that in many ways, this thousand-mile journey had been an extended meditation on joy itself—not the shallow, fleeting happiness our culture often mistakes for joy, but something deeper and more enduring. True joy, I now understood, is what emerges when we live in alignment with our authentic selves, when we pursue what calls to our hearts rather than what appeals to our egos, when we measure our worth not by others' metrics but by our own deepest values. In this triumphant moment of reaching mile 1,000, I imagined sharing the news with Celeste, and her response seemed to float on the breeze:

Dear Brenda,

A thousand miles! Not just traveled, but chosen, walked, and now claimed as your own. In a world that constantly tells us what success should look like, you carved your own path and followed it to completion. This journey was never about proving anything to the world—it was about remembering who you truly are.

The joy you feel now is the purest kind—born not from crossing a finish line others have drawn, but from honoring the call of your own heart. It cannot be replicated through shortcuts or substitutes. It comes only from authentic challenge embraced with your whole being.

That roadrunner who greeted you at mile 999 recognized a kindred spirit—one who moves at her own pace, navigates by her own compass, and finds her way through landscapes others might fear to traverse alone. Nature has been your witness all along, but more importantly, you have been your own witness—seeing, acknowledging, and celebrating each step of your becoming.

Carry this hard-earned joy forward as your talisman. When future paths seem unclear or conventional wisdom would pull you off course, remember this feeling. Remember that true joy comes when you follow your own star, set your own pace, and recognize your own arrival.

With boundless pride in your journey,

Celeste

When I began this quest, I was searching—for purpose, for direction, for a way to navigate this chapter of my life. I had wanted to prove to myself that age was just a number, that I could still embrace adventure and challenge. But somewhere between mile 1 and mile 1,000, this journey became about so much more than physical endurance or arbitrary goals. It became a pilgrimage to my own center, a way of learning to trust my instincts again, to listen to the quiet voice within that had been drowned out by expectations and "shoulds."

I thought about the many lessons the trail had taught me. How to navigate by instinct when the path wasn't clear. How to find shelter in unexpected places. How to appreciate the journey rather than fixating on the destination. How to recognize when pushing forward was courage and when it was folly. These weren't just hiking skills—they were life skills, wisdom I would carry with me long after the trail dust had been washed away.

Perhaps the true test of this journey's impact lies not in completing the thousand miles, but in how I live all the miles that follow. Will I continue to walk paths of my own choosing? Will I measure my worth by my own standards rather than society's? Will I remember that true joy comes not from external validation but from living authentically?

As I close this chapter, I feel a profound sense of gratitude—for the trails that carried me, the challenges that shaped me, the people who supported me, and the inner voice that guided me home to myself. One thousand miles behind me, a lifetime of adventures ahead. The joy of authentic living continues, one step at a time.

22.

TRAIL MARKERS OF SUCCESS

True success is living in alignment with your values—where joy, resilience, and authenticity outweigh external validation. It's not a destination but a daily choice, a commitment to releasing society's expectations in favor of a life that feels true.

~

SUCCESS, HOWEVER YOU DEFINE IT, REQUIRES A PLAN!

WHEN I SET out on my 1,000-mile quest, I had spreadsheets, maps, and a structured itinerary. But life doesn't follow tidy formulas. Some days brought storms, exhaustion, or unexpected detours. Success, I learned, is a balance between structure and flexibility—rigid plans snap under pressure, while aimlessness leads nowhere. The key is creating a framework that provides direction while allowing room for discovery.

SUCCESS IS DEVOTING TIME TO YOURSELF WITHOUT GUILT OR APOLOGY.

Early on, I struggled with guilt. Who was I to dedicate five months to personal growth? That guilt came from deep-seated beliefs that worth is measured by productivity. But as the miles added up, I reframed my journey as a sabbatical—an intentional pause for renewal. I wasn't shirking responsibility; I was honoring it. Self-care isn't selfish—it's necessary for growth.

SUCCESS IS BUILDING OPPORTUNITIES FROM FAILURE.

Business setbacks had shaken my confidence, but the trail taught me to see failure as a redirection rather than a dead end. Steep switchbacks often doubled back before leading to higher ground—life works the same way. What looks like retreat is sometimes the necessary route to progress.

SUCCESS IS EMBRACING THE FREEDOM OF "ENOUGH."

We're conditioned to chase more—more money, achievements, possessions. But the pursuit of "more" can be a treadmill that never stops. Growing up with little, I feared scarcity. Ironically, that fear kept me trapped. The trail showed me that "enough" is a mindset, not a number. It's choosing sufficiency over excess, experience over accumulation.

SUCCESS IS DARING TO BECOME.

Evolution isn't linear—it happens in leaps and plateaus. Finding an old sticky note where I had written about feeling "half the person I want to be" was a wake-up call. I had grown without even realizing it. Success isn't about meeting someone else's standard—it's about stepping fully into your own authenticity.

SUCCESS IS FACING YOUR FEARS.

A rattlesnake on the trail reminded me that fear isn't to be avoided but understood. Every time I crossed a ridge or faced uncertainty, I expanded my boundaries. Fear of judgment, financial insecurity, loneliness—each one lost its grip when confronted. The greatest treasures lie just beyond the places that scare us most.

SUCCESS IS EMBRACING SOLITUDE.

Society equates solitude with loneliness, but the wilderness taught me otherwise. In the quiet miles, I discovered that solitude isn't something to endure—it's a gift. Like Dorothy Molter, the Root Beer Lady, I found that being alone deepens self-knowledge. Wholeness doesn't come from others—it starts within.

SUCCESS IS UNBECOMING.

Becoming is powerful, but so is shedding—letting go of conditioned beliefs, outdated expectations, and false identities. Standing at Crater Lake, I realized my journey wasn't just about gaining wisdom; it was about unburdening myself from "shoulds" and "musts." Nature doesn't separate work from play, doesn't measure worth by status. Returning to my true self was as important as evolving into something new.

SUCCESS IS CHOOSING YOUR ENERGY.

Like the Rogue River, shifting between rapids and calm pools, I realized that we shape our reality through the energy we bring. The grumbling hiker on Garfield Peak and the joyful couple sliding down snow at Wizard Island experienced the same landscape—filtered through their attitudes. Choosing our energy is an act of personal power, not forced positivity but intentional presence.

SUCCESS IS RELEASING EXPECTATIONS.

As a parent, I had clung to expectations, unknowingly placing a burden on my son—and myself. On the bleak trails of the Olympic Peninsula, I saw that true love and success come from releasing the need to control outcomes. People, like trails, have their own natural course. Our job isn't to mold them, but to honor their path.

SUCCESS IS FINDING COURAGE TO THRIVE AT LIFE'S BOUNDARIES.

The richest biodiversity exists at boundaries—where ecosystems meet. Likewise, the most profound growth happens at life's edges—where comfort meets challenge, where certainty meets the unknown. My time in Washington reinforced this. The Bluff Trail's sudden transition from dense forest to ocean vista showed that sometimes, we must push through darkness to find light. Even painful experiences—like the dog bite that left me scarred—became catalysts for growth.

SUCCESS LIES IN SURRENDERING CONTROL.

Perhaps the hardest lesson is knowing when to hold on and when to let go. Our culture glorifies control—over circumstances, others, even ourselves—feeding the illusion that we dictate life's course. But surrender isn't passive resignation; it's an active choice to stop resisting and start flowing. It's not abandoning responsibility but recognizing our limits and directing energy where it matters. True success comes not from forcing outcomes but from making peace with uncertainty and embracing what unfolds.

23.

TRAIL MARKERS OF JOY

Joy is the radiance that emerges when we fully engage with life—discovering wonder in nature, strength in challenges, meaning in connection, and peace in our own rhythm. It thrives on curiosity and presence, expanding through genuine relationships, and outlasts us as we share it with others—an eternal dance of light, like fireflies illuminating a summer night.

~

SOMETIMES JOY DISAPPEARS IN THE MIST.

THE RELENTLESS GLOOM of the Olympic Peninsula taught me that joy, like sunshine, can be temporarily obscured. For weeks, I trudged through dense forests where light barely penetrated, my spirits sinking with each gray, dripping day. I had expected exhilaration, the kind I had felt through California's mountains and Oregon's forests, but instead, I found myself disconnected, as if joy had abandoned me.

What saved me wasn't resisting the absence of joy but surrendering to it. I stopped demanding constant bliss and began honoring the full spectrum of emotions the journey evoked. Some days would shine with clarity and excitement; others would be steeped in doubt and fatigue. Both had value. When joy finally reemerged—watching fields of fireweed scatter their seeds like summer snowflakes—it was more vivid for having been lost. I realized that joy's disappearance wasn't failure; it was part of its natural rhythm, like the tides or the seasons. Absence makes presence more precious. Joy is a rhythm we learn to trust, knowing it will always return.

JOY THRIVES IN SIMPLICITY.

The lighthouse keepers' singular focus—maintaining the beacon that guided ships to safety—illuminated a profound truth: joy flourishes in the soil of simplicity. Their lives stood in stark contrast to my own, where I had long juggled multiple projects, measuring success by productivity rather than presence.

Standing in that lantern room, gazing over the Strait of Juan de Fuca, I saw how joy doesn't emerge from doing everything, but from doing what matters most with complete presence. Society rewards multitasking, but nature teaches us that focus creates power. A lighthouse beam doesn't try to illuminate the entire ocean; it cuts through fog by shining steadily on what is essential. I began to see how simplifying my focus—whether on writing, nature, or nourishing connections—might concentrate my joy, making it more potent and enduring than when scattered across too many pursuits. True joy is found in the unburdened moments, when we strip away the unnecessary and embrace life's simplest gifts.

JOY GROWS THROUGH CONNECTION.

Like the edges where ecosystems meet—those fertile boundaries described at the Chinese Gardens—connections create conditions where joy flourishes in unexpected abundance. Throughout my journey, I've found that joy expands when shared, whether with strangers, loved ones, or the wild creatures that cross my path.

The women on the Centennial Trail illustrated this perfectly. What could have been a moment of awkwardness—our near collision on the path—turned into spontaneous joy when I playfully declared, "Well, since you're walking on my side of the trail, you must want a hug." Her surprised laughter, followed by a genuine embrace, transformed the moment into something magical, dissolving cultural barriers.

These connections extend beyond humans. The hummingbird hovering near my head, the bobcat appearing at dusk three nights in a row, the roadrunner darting across my path at mile 999—each encounter wove me into the larger fabric of life. Even Celeste, whom I met for just one afternoon years ago, remains a presence in my life, her wisdom guiding me through miles of uncertainty. Joy is not a solitary pursuit; it's an energy exchanged, a thread that links us to something greater. The more we share joy, the more it multiplies, echoing long after the moment has passed.

CURIOSITY IS THE INSTIGATOR OF JOY.

"What's around the next bend?" That question has propelled me forward countless times, urging me to continue when exhaustion tempted me to stop. Whether hiking to Preston Falls, exploring an unmarked trail, or wandering into a small-town museum, curiosity has been my most steadfast companion.

This instinct extends beyond physical exploration. When I noticed a mastodon painted among cattle in a mural in Sequim, I had to know why. Learning about the 1977 discovery of mastodon bones in a local farmer's field connected me to the deep history of the land, an unexpected delight. Children embody this mindset naturally—every leaf holds a secret, every stone a possibility. But somewhere along the way, many of us trade curiosity for certainty, choosing comfort over discovery.

Yet the trail has taught me that joy lives in the questions, not the answers. It thrives when we take unfamiliar turns, talk to strangers, or pause to examine what we'd normally pass by. Joy isn't just found at the summit—it's in the mystery of the next step. To remain joyful, we must remain curious, seeing the world not as a collection of known facts, but as an unfolding wonder waiting to be explored.

JOY IS MAKING PEACE WITH THE PASSAGE OF TIME.

The Oregon coast became my teacher in temporal wisdom as I watched the shoreline transform with each tide. At low tide, the beach stretched endlessly, inviting exploration. Hours later, the same expanse disappeared beneath rushing waters, altering the landscape entirely. It was a daily lesson in impermanence.

In youth, life feels like perpetual low tide—time stretching infinitely before us. The middle years accelerate, responsibilities rushing in like high tide, leaving us gasping, "Where did the time go?" Now, no longer in life's middle, I walk the transition zone—some days catching the last stretch of low tide, other days stepping back as the waters rise. The footprints I once left in the sand now vanish more quickly. But instead of fighting time's passage, I find peace in embracing it. We don't own time; we are its temporary custodians, and joy comes in choosing how we leave our mark before the tide returns. Rather than fearing the tide's advance, I find joy in the ever-changing rhythm of time's dance.

POSSIBILITIES ARE THE GATEWAY TO JOY.

While gazing at the Hunter's Moon hanging brilliantly over the Oregon coast, I realized that possibilities open doorways to our deepest joys. They appear not as grand revelations, but as quiet messages—easily missed without receptivity. The shared lunar moment with my son, the 4 a.m. epiphany about working in nature, the unexpected connection with hiking strangers—none were dramatic events, but each illuminated pathways to joy.

These possibilities present themselves in various forms. Possibilities of connection, like the supermoon linking me to my son across miles, reminding me that shared wonder transcends distance. Possibilities of reinvention, like my pre-dawn realization about working as a nature guide, arriving not through careful planning but in the liminal space between consciousness and dreams. And possibilities of authentic living, like shedding the expectations tied to age and status that had unknowingly anchored me to limitations.

What makes these possibilities transformative is their personal resonance—they can't be forced or fabricated. They emerge in moments of stillness and receptivity, carrying invitations we might otherwise dismiss. Joy doesn't require grand achievements. Sometimes, it waits within a possibility we've been too constrained to consider. In a world fixated on certainties, joy reveals itself through openness to the unexpected, reminding us that our greatest fulfillment often lies just beyond the boundaries we've accepted as fixed.

JOY IS REBELLIOUS.

In the wilderness of the Rogue River, cut off from constant connectivity, I learned that choosing joy is an act of rebellion in a world that thrives on outrage and anxiety. When the news cycle, social media, and politics profit from our distress, deliberately protecting our joy becomes a radical stance. It's not about ignorance but about resisting the forces that feed on division, refusing to let them dominate our emotional state. By nurturing inner peace, we become more resilient, grounded, and effective in fighting for what matters.

Joy defies the noise and negativity around us, especially in politics. In a world where fear and anger are manipulated for power, allowing them to consume us only makes us easier to control. A joyful, centered person—one who can take action without losing herself—is the truest rebellion. By setting boundaries around political engagement and unplugging from the digital world, I reclaimed my days and my joy, refusing to let the toxic rhetoric rob me of my strength and clarity. In this rage-fueled world, choosing joy is revolutionary.

JOY IS FORGED IN ADVERSITY AND RESILIENCE.

Joy, like the growth rings of a tree, is shaped not in perfect conditions but through struggle. The hardest, strongest rings in a tree's trunk form in times of drought, when the tree must fight for every drop of water. Similarly, the greatest joys of my journey weren't in easy moments but in those that challenged me. Facing a rattlesnake or enduring the heat at Eastman Lake didn't provide instant pleasure, but they gave me a deeper, more resilient joy—the kind that arises from overcoming adversity.

True joy isn't about comfort; it's about the strength that comes from perseverance. Just as metal must be forged in fire, joy reaches its fullest form through challenge. Each test on my journey deepened my capacity for joy, revealing a satisfaction that no smooth path could have provided. The trials I faced weren't obstacles to joy but the very thing that made it profound and lasting. By the time I neared my thousandth mile, I understood that the joy of the journey wasn't despite the challenges, but because of them.

TRUE JOY COMES FROM CROSSING YOUR OWN FINISH LINE.

When I reached mile 1,000, the joy I felt wasn't just about the achievement itself but about proving to myself that I could set an audacious goal and complete it, one step at a time. It wasn't about external validation, but the confidence in my own strength and clarity. The joy came from knowing I had walked my own path, overcome limiting beliefs, and stayed true to my values throughout the journey.

Each of us has a unique finish line. Whether it's climbing a mountain, writing a book, or simply getting through a tough day, true joy springs from honoring our own journey. My thousand-mile trek wasn't about impressing others; it was about reconnecting with myself, proving that age is just a number, and finding clarity amidst life's chaos. The joy at the finish line came from knowing I had remained true to my intentions, and that joy, like the roadrunner at mile 999, was about moving at my own pace and embracing my unique essence.

EPILOGUE

WITHIN A WEEK of returning to my winter home, I had a job lined up for the summer. I will step into a new role as an ATV guide, leading adventurers through towering groves of ponderosa pines to the rim of Bryce Canyon National Park, in Utah. I'll share the story of the hoodoos—those otherworldly spires of red rock sculpted by time and the elements—and help eager eyes spot pronghorn as they move like whispers across the ancient landscape. My home will be in the employee campground, where I'll be part of another community, surrounded by nature's masterpiece, paid to share the wonders I love. My spirit soars just thinking about it.

But joy and sorrow often walk hand in hand. My elation is bittersweet. Mom won't be here to share in my stories.

On October 17th, mom celebrated her 92nd birthday. She giggled as she told me about her lunch out with the girls at the restaurant that offered a birthday special—matching its discount with the number of years. Mom received a 92% discount off her filet mignon! Her delight at this small windfall sparkled through the phone, a moment of humor amid increasingly difficult days.

By November 4th, we made the heartbreaking decision to move her into assisted living. The farmhouse that had held a lifetime of memories—the home where she raised her children, where holidays unfolded in warmth and laughter—could no longer support her growing needs.

Yet even in this transition, Mom found a way to thrive. She reunited with neighbors from decades past, formed new friendships, and, with characteristic resilience, brightened every room she entered. But time was running out.

On a sunny November day, I boarded a plane to Minneapolis. I stepped off into a world of ice and snow, then made my way to the old farmhouse in central Wisconsin. Over the next ten days, I spent every moment I could with Mom—massaging her feet, helping her write her last story, pushing her wheelchair to the piano, sharing memories.

I watched her fade. On my 61st birthday, I knew we were near the end. That day, I wheeled her in front of the piano—her lifelong joy. Her fingers, frail but determined, found their way to the keys. The melody of "Happy Birthday" filled the air, trembling but true, like her spirit—unyielding, beautiful. In that moment, where she had spent so many days receiving care, I wanted her to feel the joy of giving again.

When the final note faded, I knelt beside her wheelchair and took her hands in mine. "Thank you for being a wonderful mother," I whispered, my voice catching. "I love you."

"I love you too," she said, her grip stronger than I expected, pulling me into one last embrace.

We both knew it was the last. As I stepped away, her tears mirrored mine. I made my exit, carrying her love like a beacon.

The bus was late. Snow-covered ground glistened under streetlights as I waited in my sister's car, the heater humming against the cold. When the bus finally arrived, I stepped out into the biting air, hugged my sister tight, and joined a few quiet strangers at the depot. I took a window seat, darkness swallowing the road ahead. As the miles stretched between us, silent tears slipped down my cheeks. I had been given a rare gift—the chance to say goodbye, a gift not everyone receives. I thought of my thousand-mile journey—each step taking me somewhere new while tethering me to what matters most.

On December 21, my brother called. "Mom died early this morning."

I was in the Sonoran Desert, midway through a ranger-led hike. I stepped away from the group, watching my tears darken the dry sand. But then, gratitude. Mom had lived 92 years. She had been given time. We had been given time.

That evening, as the sun melted into the mountains, I felt something profound shift within me. The saguaros, standing sentinel for centuries, bore witness to life's endless cycles—birth, growth, death, renewal. These ancient plants had endured the harshest conditions for hundreds of years, their very existence a testament to resilience and patience.

In that stark and silent desert, surrounded by life that had learned to thrive in seeming emptiness, I found an unexpected comfort—raw, honest, enduring. Mom's energy hadn't disappeared but transformed, just as the desert transforms rain into vibrant, if brief, blooms. Her influence remained in how I saw the world, in the courage I'd found to live authentically, in the capacity for joy she'd modeled even in her final days.

The grief was real, a hollow space that would remain. But so was the gratitude—for our final moments together, for her lasting gifts, for the wisdom to recognize that endings make way for beginnings. I realized that completing my thousand-mile journey just months before her life journey ended wasn't coincidence but convergence—two paths meeting at the intersection of letting go and moving forward.

Death brings clarity. What truly matters? What lights me up inside? I knew one thing for certain—I was done with my financial coaching business. I wasn't walking away from a struggle; I was stepping into something truer. That chapter had drained me, pulled me away from the life I wanted. With that decision, a door swung open—to more writing, more travel, more adventure. To a life that made me feel alive.

Back in California, surrounded by the vastness of the high desert, I finally understood what had drawn me to Celeste on that ferry. That quiet radiance, that deep peace with her choices—it wasn't just something she carried. It was something she passed on. And in those final moments with Mom, I felt it in myself. A peace with my own life, my own choices. I would carry Mom's spirit with me, and Celeste's energy had become woven into my story.

I want to carry this joy to my final breath. I want to be remembered as the woman on the trail, the woman in the RV, or maybe, the woman on the ATV— the one who inspired others to live fully, deeply, without apology.

Through this journey, I've learned that we all leave ripples in the world— through our energy, our joy, our way of being. Just as Celeste's brief presence in my life created lasting waves of transformation, maybe my own path will touch others in ways I'll never fully know.

What I do know is that somewhere along the way, my fear of death changed. I used to be terrified of dying alone, of dying broke, of fading without family or friends. But that fear no longer holds me. Instead of dreading a lonely, painful end, I now imagine something softer, something full of grace.

I see myself in an Adirondack chair as the sun sinks behind the horizon. The full moon rises over a still lake, fireflies flickering like tiny lanterns. A fleece blanket shields me from the evening chill as I listen to the symphony of tree frogs, the crackle of distant campfires. And when I take my last breath, my energy drifts away on firefly wings, dispersing into the night sky.

But for now, my journey continues. Each day is an invitation—to share joy, to inspire, to live with reckless wonder. And maybe that's the greatest lesson of all—that joy isn't just something we feel. It's something we pass on. A light that grows brighter with every heart it touches, dancing eternal, like fireflies on a summer night.

Like fireflies on a summer night, we shine briefly but brilliantly. Our light mingles with others, creating patterns more beautiful than any single glow could achieve alone. And though individual lights fade, the dance continues—an unbroken rhythm between darkness and radiance, solitude and connection, what passes and what endures.

This is my mother's legacy. This is Celeste's gift. This is my continuing journey.

And the trail stretches on before me, calling me forward into whatever adventure awaits.

ABOUT THE AUTHOR

Dr. Brenda K. Uekert is a sociologist, writer, and adventurer, who inspires others to find joy, freedom, and authenticity. A full-time RVer and avid hiker, Brenda traded a conventional life for a journey of exploration and self-discovery. When she's not on the road traveling with her cats, Brenda enjoys a winter base in southern California.